The Way It Was According to Chick

Growing Up on the Spokane Indian Reservation

by

Robert "Chick" Wynecoop

Tornado Creek Publications

P.O. Box 8625
Spokane, WA 99203
(509) 838-7114

Published in 2003
Printed in the United States of America
by

Library of Congress Control Number: 2003106594
ISBN 0974088102

Tornado Creek Publications
P.O. Box 8625
Spokane, WA 99203

About the Author

Bob "Chick" Wynecoop was born at Wellpinit, Washington November 3, 1935 in a log cabin. He attended grades 1-12 at Wellpinit Grade and High School, graduating high school in 1954. He attended and graduated from Washington State (now WSU) College with a degree in Forestry in 1958. He enlisted in the U.S. Army and served for 33 months as an instructor in photo mapping at the U. S. Army Engineer School at Fort Belvoir, Virginia.

Bob Wynecoop

Following his term in the army, he worked for the U. S. Department of Agriculture at Coram, Big Prairie and Glacier View Ranger Districts on the Flathead National Forest, the regional office in Missoula, and the Forest Supervisor's office in Helena, Montana, where he met Lois, his wife-to-be. They were later transferred to the Clearwater National Forest supervisor's office in Orofino, Idaho. During Bob's career, he also worked at the following places: Canyon Ranger District also on the Clearwater; the Troy Ranger District, on the Kootenai National Forest; the supervisor's office on the Kootenai in Libby Montana; the regional office in Missoula, Montana (again); The Department of Interior Bureau of Indian Affairs, Portland Area Office, Portland Ore; and the planning branch at Denver, Colorado. Bob ended up as the Chief of Natural Resources at the Minneapolis Area Office, Minneapolis, Minnesota. He retired in 1994, returning to Spokane Washington in September of 2001. His hobbies are running, backpacking and hunting.

Lois and Bob have two children. Their daughter Kerry Kulus and her husband Steve, who live in St. Cloud, Minnesota, have a daughter, Kaylee Ann. Kerry is a registered nurse. Their son Keith has a performing arts degree and is currently working as a performer in a national touring show.

Dedication

I dedicate this book to my beautiful and loving wife Lois, not only in appreciation for her help with this book, but mainly for being my best friend and soul-mate.

Acknowledgements

This book started when my children, Kerry and Keith, asked their Grandma Doris Bentzen to fill out a booklet on her childhood. This sparked my recollections of stories of when I grew up on the Spokane Indian Reservation. One story led to another resulting in this book which, in my wildest dreams, I never thought I would write, let alone publish.

There are many people who deserve recognition for this project: My parents Clair and Phoebe Wynecoop, who brought me to this world. I thank them for allowing me to grow up as a country boy, giving me the freedom to roam the hills along the Spokane River, and have many fun adventures.

I especially appreciate and thank my wife Lois for her support and encouragement to start and finish this text. Without her encouragement and computer knowledge I would have never started or completed this book.

I thank Suzanne Kita of Crystal Clear Communications, Bailey, Colorado, who was willing to take on the initial critique and edit of this book. Also Tony and Suzanne Bamonte of Tornado Creek Publications for making this book a reality. It is one thing to put words on paper and another to produce a book and I thank them for their help.

I thank Tina Wynecoop for her assistance with the foreword and connecting us with the Bamontes and my thanks to all the people who provided pictures. They are credited with each photo.

TABLE OF CONTENTS

Foreword

Introduction

1. Wild Neighbors 16
2. The Radio 18
3. The Mouse That Roared 22
4. Tree Games 24
5. Chores Galore 31
6. Playing Outside 37
7. Adventures-A-Plenty 39
8. Hay Play 42
9. First Smokes 45
10. Grandparents 50
11. Clothes for the Day and Beds for the Night 55
12. Dick Is Lost 57
13. Bucked Off 59
14. Riding Pigs 61
15. Electric Fence 62
16. Childhood Diseases 64
17. Starting School 66
18. Chewing Gum 76
19. Picking Berries 79
20. Preparing for War 82
21. Christmas Celebrations 83
22. School Activities 88
23. Water Problems 93
24. Summer Chores 96
25. Mose is Stranded 100
26. More New Chores 102
27. Feeding Cattle and Chasing Strays 105
28. Sled Riding 107
29. Walt's White Thing and Other Scary Stuff 109
30. Ice Skating 112
31. Winter Haystacks 115
32. Sleepwalking 117
33. Playing in the House 119
34. Construction Projects 123
35. Bible School 126
36. The Milk Cow 128
37. Riding Horses 131
38. Playing With Friends 138
39. Trapping and Hunting 145
40 A Fishing Tale 152
41. More Homemade Toys and Gun Tales 156
42. Forest Fires, More Smoking, and Chewing, Too 163
43. Corrals and Barns 167
44. Hauling Hay 171
45. Sleeping in the Bushes 175
46. Graveyards, Outhouses, Uncle Roy and Halloween 176
47. Ponds and Rafts 179
48. Swimming 181
49. The Electric Club and the B-29 Crash 185
50. Political Conventions 190
51. Eating Meals, "Wild" Snacks and P.J. 191
52. Hotshot Slingshots 195
53. Baseball 197
54. Spokane Trips 201
55. The Telephone 204
56. Tex Does His Thing 208
57. Spring on the Spokane River 210
58 Movies Here and There 217
59. While the Folks Were Away 219
60. Dad Becomes a Pilot 220
61. Home Movies 222

My Home

by William A. Galbraith

There's a place that is known to a few alone

Where the great wide forests span

"Tis the home and place of a dying race,
the real American

There's beauty there that fills the air
with inspiration real

And one may see in the land so free
the thing that others feel

Where'er I roam I'll find no home
so dear in any nation

As the home I've known out there alone

On the Spokane Reservation

THE SPOKANE INDIAN RESERVATION

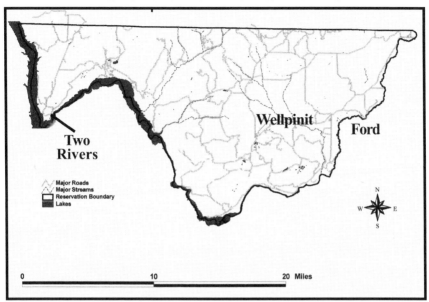

The Spokane Reservation was created in January 1881 by President Rutherford B. Hayes. *(Map courtesy Bureau of Indian Affairs)*

"Two Rivers Casino & Resort" located at the southwestern portion of the Spokane Indian Reservation, where the Columbia and Spokane Rivers come together. "Two Rivers" is one of the most beautiful and well-maintained recreational areas in the State.

Foreword

It is not surprising that a childhood rich with adventure - experienced while growing up on an Indian reservation - would result in this book. Chick (almost everyone gets a nickname among tribal people) or Bob, as he is known off the reservation, is simply carrying on the telling of his stories in the tribe's oral tradition. He comes from a family of story- tellers. Had all six of his brothers lived to retirement age, they too would have had time to write of their own childhood experiences, and filled six more books!

Chick's next older brother, Judge (Arnold), has been putting his own memories on paper for years - hoping to get his finished first because "his version of the way things happened is the correct one". Being competitive, Chick reached the publisher ahead of him. Another brother, Dave, authored a history of the Spokane tribe called, *Children of the Sun*: A History of the Spokane Indians. It is still in print, though Dave's untimely death has silenced his voice.

Telling stories *The Way It Was According to Chick* is akin to the way elders would enliven long winter nights - teaching lessons, traditions, history, creation myths, and much, much more, through the familiar and eagerly anticipated medium of story. When the seasons changed and days lengthened, food gathering, tool making, hunting and travel were paramount, so the stories were tucked away for a while, but not forgotten. Chick, too, left these marvelous experiences tucked in his memory until retirement - the "winter" of his life - provided time to leave a written record.

One of Chick's grandmothers, Nancy Perkins Wynecoop, was born at Tshimikain Mission near Ford, Washington. She was a Lakes Indian, from a tribe that inhabited the headwaters of the Columbia River. The nomadic nature of the Interior Salish peoples explains her family's eventual settlement so far south of their traditional grounds. She was adopted into the Spokane Tribe and given land to live on along the river. She too was a writer, telling the stories of her grandmother Seepetza (Able One), only to have her manuscripts destroyed in three separate house fires. Finally, she gave her fourth manuscript for the book to the library of the Eastern Washington State Historical Society for safekeeping. Her daughter, Nettie Wynecoop Clark published it in 1985 with the title: *In The Stream: An Indian Story*.

Nancy's son Clair (Cil-Speelya, "five coyotes") received his name because someone gave him a tanned coyote hide as a gift when he was a baby and that is what he slept on. And, I might add, that Wig (George), his oldest son, received his name because his granddad called him "Chief Wigame" when he was little, while Judge (Arnold) was given his because he always looked at things so seriously, as if he was really worried. Chick was named after a wrestler named Bob Robert Chick, according to his mom, but Judge and Chick remember that his ribcage looked like a chicken's. (When Chick had his first health examination the tribe's physician, Dr. Stevenson, considered him a "perfect baby".) Vern (or Wade) the seventh son loved to listen to Red Foley's songs when he was little and since he pronounced Red's last name "Fody", he acquired the name "Fody". Three sons, Steve, Dave and Dick did not get additional names because their father said he was going to choose names for them so that they wouldn't get nicknamed - using names that in his mind were already nicknames.

Their dad, Clair, charismatic and energetic, established a cattle ranch that his sons managed. He gave them many responsibilities, trusting if they all worked hard and contributed to the family business they would keep out of trouble. (This memoir reveals he may have miscalculated.) He also owned a logging company, was president of the richest uranium mine in the northwest, and was one of the founders of The Northwest Affiliated Tribes/United American Indians organizations along with Levi McCormack, the famed Nez Perce baseball star. Clair was an elected tribal judge and served as council chairman. He had a profound influence on the reservation and his family.

Chick's mother, Phoebe Galbraith Wynecoop, (aged 94), has been keeping a daily journal for over 40 years, recording a full and active life still in progress. Phoebe is the first Spokane tribal member to become a schoolteacher. She graduated from Cheney Normal School and returned with her certificate to instruct the children of her own tribe. One of her grandfathers was the first territorial judge of Montana. Her Scottish and

Indian heritage, her strong ethics and quiet strength, enabled her to raise seven sons well. She fostered keen skills of observation and remembrance in her children, who all claim that few mothers have given their children happier childhoods.

I hope the reader enjoys this book as much as I have. It is written by someone of mixed-blood with feet in two worlds - growing up in a time of prejudice towards Indians, when it was safer to be non-Indian if one wanted to "succeed". Chick came of age during that unique era which followed on the heels of the Great Depression and included World War II. He is the third son in a family of boys who were so innocent that when tourists came by busloads from nearby Spokane to "see the Indians" on the Spokane Indian Reservation, they and their tribal friends ran after the buses to "see the Indians" too. At the time, none of them realized that where they grew up, who their friends and companions were, and how lovingly they were cared for, would provide that fertile ground needed to produce these marvelous stories.

Tina Wynecoop ("Miss Granmo") - 2003

The Wynecoop family in 1948. Standing: Dick, Dave, Chick, and Steve. Seated: Judge, Phoebe, Vern, Clair and Wig. *(Photo by Athow Studio)*

INTRODUCTION

According to Mom, it was a miserable, cold evening on November 3, 1935, when I was born. The local Indian Health doctor who assisted with the delivery was slightly inebriated when he arrived at the folks' small log home on the Spokane Indian Reservation in the foothills of eastern Washington State. Accounts of his less-than-sober state must have been true because he failed to register my birth, which caused me a few problems later in life.

I grew up in what would be eventually a family of seven boys, all born and raised on the Reservation at a time and location where we were part of the "locals," and that was all we needed to be. We did our thing and no one bothered us.

Like most kids growing up in the country in the late 1930s, I thought it was a great time to be a kid. The Great Depression still had most of the country in a tight grip, but we were too young to know that times were tough. We always had plenty of food to eat and each other to play with. We started school just before or during the early years of World War II. Because of the war effort, toys, candy, and other "kid things" were not part of our everyday life, so we really didn't miss something we never had and did not know existed. Sure, there were a few things like chewing gum that we couldn't enjoy often, but we adjusted and developed substitutes.

We learned the importance of work and developed a strong work ethic early on. We also learned to help support the family "team." We all pitched in, and generally, everyone pulled his share to get through the hard times. We never waited to be asked; we were taught to just jump in and help. In the process, we did many things few kids would do today, and we had fun along the way.

Most of my tales are memories that resulted from many kitchen and dining room talk sessions where, as adults, we would sit down and tell stories about growing up. We laughed so hard about some of the things that happened that I decided to write down my "middle child" memories.

As the middle child, the third of 7 boys, I had the chance to run with the older ones, yet still do things with the younger ones, too. Mom's kitchen table was where we'd congregate and visit, both as kids and as adults. What a time we had – and still have – together at our family gatherings!

Now, when we find ourselves back in Mom's kitchen, one of the surviving brothers will start a story. Then each of us adds his version and the laughter begins. Other family members wander into the small kitchen to listen to our many tales. It is worth the price of admission just to enjoy the laughter of people who have lived great lives, remember the real stories, and share them freely.

Most of the events that happened are hard to put a date on, but this is my version of the stories. Little effort is made to keep things in chronological order, but there is some order, because as we got older, we took on more responsibility and did different chores.

There were always plenty of chores to do; they were just part of growing up. At first our chores were simple. Then, as we got older, we moved into the use of complicated equipment, driving tractors, and riding horses.

The first stories are the adventures of the three older boys: George a.k.a. "Wig," Arnold a.k.a. "Judge," and Robert a.k.a. "Chick." We each had a nickname, and everyone else in our small community had nicknames, too.

We lived near the little town of Wellpinit, Washington, on the Spokane Indian Reservation. Spokane was the nearest city of any size, and as we grew up, it was only a distant part of our lives. We lived and played on the Reservation, which during World War II was pretty quiet. All the young men had gone into the military service and many of the families moved away to find work.

The core of the Reservation's activities were the church, school, and the Sub-Agency, which employed four to ten people, depending on the season of the year. The Sub-Agency area was laid out in a circle with houses, a garage, the jail, the medical clinic and the office on the outside edge of the road surrounding the open field in the center of the Agency. There was also a wooden sidewalk between the houses and the road on three-fourths of the circle.

On one edge of the circle was an old icehouse filled with ice that was buried in sawdust for insulation. Not too far from the Agency was the local general store and post office. That is where we went for information and gossip about the community. That's where I learned important news of the outside world, like when President Roosevelt died in 1945.

The town of Wellpinit was small, but still had grades one through twelve in the public school. The roads were not paved, and we were too far away to be bused to a neighboring town school. One year, our school had only one

The Spokane Indian Sub-Agency at Wellipinit in the 1930s. *(Photo courtesy Dot Tandy)*

high school senior. The average class had four to six students, and the whole high school had a total of 22-26 students. There were four of us in my 1954 graduating class.

In our early years, we lived a fun-filled full life, and played in the surrounding area – heavily timbered rolling hills with some land cleared for housing and farming, dotted here and there with large natural meadows.

This was a great place for raising a family. As we started school, our little world expanded to include many new friends and adventures. Some of our adventures were life-threatening, but somehow we survived.

Dad built a new house on a piece of land we owned, but, since we were at the end of the Depression, money was tight. He hired help and traded services for other help during the construction.

The land we owned was most of one of the meadows, suitable and ready for farming. I believe it took a year or so to build the new house. In 1941, we moved into this larger house that had four bedrooms – three upstairs – but no running water.

Left row starting at front to back: Chuck Tandy, Russell Eddy, Darrel Hastings, Philip Wynecoop, Edith Williams, Pauline Abrahamson, Kathleen Stearns, Dutch Thatcher, Second row: Nancy Ignace, Dorothy Wynne, Helen Eddy, Sonny Campbell, Marlene Wynne, Thomas Sam, Chick Wynecoop, Maryanne Sherwood, Mr. Estes. Third row: Jim Wynne, Mel Peone, Kenneth Eddy, Carson Sherwood and Glenn Galbraith. *(Highschool photo from 1952 school yearbook)*

Wig, Chick and Judge "all dressed up." *(Phoebe Wynecoop photo)*

The folks sold the log house when we moved into the new one, which was located on the south side of town. Mom lives there to this day. The old log house was about a mile away on the north side, and later burned to the ground. What a big move – a whole mile across our Reservation's universe!

That old log house never had running water. We finally got electricity for it in 1939. I guess by modern standards, it was quite primitive, but to us kids, we didn't know the difference. That's just the way we lived.

Back before we had electricity, I can remember trying to light a kerosene lantern. Kerosene lamps did not produce much light, even with a clean chimney. If you didn't have the wick adjusted right, the glass quickly sooted up and turned black. Of course, this blocked the light and defeated your purpose. Then you had to take off the sooty glass, clean it, and hope you didn't soot it up again. After several aborted efforts by us kids, Mom or Dad usually solved the problem without our help.

Our outside toilet had a quarter moon cut in the door and a mail order catalog to use for toilet paper. An outhouse was really something, especially when it was cold. After dark, anything was legal. Visiting the outhouse on business after dark could be a real adventure. While a lantern or flashlight made the trip a little easier, they still didn't make me feel adequately protected from the unknown.

Ghosts were everywhere! By the time I was safely back inside the house, I was puffing and panting from the hard run past the ghosts who lurked all along the 30-yard trail. Sometimes on cold winter nights, we didn't make it all the way to the outhouse, and the snowy path leading to it was marked with a mysterious yellow stain.

I'll begin by describing some of our many adventures which happened during the time that we were living in the old log house. Back then, I don't remember the family traveling anywhere. We didn't need to. We did go to Loon Lake. We had enough local attractions to stimulate and entertain us. We did a lot of walking and running in the woods around that house, which was reasonably close to one of the major roads. In the '30s, that part of the state was more than a little wild.

-Chapter 1-
Wild Neighbors

Some of the locals put on a real show. In their own terminology, they were "just having a good time." Horses were still commonly used as transportation up and down our roads. One of the first stories I remember involves this lively combination – of natives and horses.

One day we heard a lot of noise coming from the direction of the main road. Horses were galloping towards town, then came ripping back down that road. And there was screaming and yelling that made our ears curl. This was too much for the three of us kids to ignore. Wig, Judge and I ran up the little hill behind our house to see more of what was going on.

When the horses and riders were on the town leg of their ride, we crawled over to the edge of the road cut. Lying flat in the grass just above the road, we watched as they came roaring by – a wild bunch on horses all dressed in buckskin with feathered bonnets on their heads and long braids. What a jolt of chills they sent up and down our spines!

They rode by, screaming and yelling, then back they came! We were scared speechless. Their horses were all lathered white and wet with sweat. You could see the fire in the horses' eyes and the effort of the riders to hold them back from running even harder. Those horses were ready to run with the wind!

Wow! This spectacle was beyond belief for us kids in our normally calm, unspectacular little world. We watched them until they finally rode one last time into town. Then we crawled back through the grass and brush, jumped up and ran for the house, all charged up ourselves and full of questions. I usually couldn't keep up with Wig and Judge, but after seeing this version of the Reservation's wild west show, I beat my brothers home.

We were so excited we could hardly get any words out. Mom told us to calm down so she could make sense out of our gibberish. We saw that Mom was pretty keyed up herself, which made us even more excited.

When we were finally able to ask our questions, Mom said that those people were a bunch of locals. We didn't understand why they were wearing the buckskin outfits and the feathered head pieces. We knew about buckskin because Dad did a lot of hunting. But their outfits and feathers were something else!

When mom said they were dressed for a celebration, that meant nothing to us. Although we did not know about the show, we did know that they were wild, noisy and having fun. Trips to the outhouse after dark were even tougher for the next few weeks.

Mom also told us then that we were living on an Indian Reservation, but that went in one ear and out the other. What made a big impression on us were the outfits they wore, plus how scary they were, and how wild they were, and how much noise they could make. They could really scream, "loud enough to curdle your blood," especially the women. Since they scared and thrilled us so much, we tried to imitate them until the next big adventure came along. Of course, that didn't take long to materialize.

Phoebe "Mom" Wynecoop *(Photo courtesy Phoebe Wynecoop)*

-Chapter 2-
The Radio

Esther, one of Dad's sisters, lived across the road from our house. She had something at her place called a radio. Our family had a crystal set, but that was not a real radio, and reception was so poor on it that we didn't even try to listen to it much.

Wig and Judge really liked listening to Aunt Esther's radio. They told me all about how amazing it was – how you could hear people talking, but no one was there. Their stories about the talking voices on the radio sounded really exciting to me, but I wasn't allowed to cross the road yet.

So, I'd just sit around and think about that radio. A box from which voices came was beyond belief to me. How could that happen? This I had to see and hear for myself, but first, I had to find a way to get across the road.

After bugging Judge until he couldn't take it anymore, he finally agreed to let me follow him up to Aunt Esther's. I was so excited that I could hardly talk. Convincing Judge was the easy part. After much fretting and worry, I finally convinced the folks that Wig and Judge would help me cross the road to get to our aunt's house.

Time never passed as slowly as it did on that big day that I was to go hear the radio for the very first time. It was like having a slow-motion dream. Finally, it was time for us to go.

Up the hill, down the bank, across the road we ran, then up the bank to our then favorite aunt's house. We burst into Aunt Esther's parlor where the radio was. It was turned on, and everything that Wig and Judge had said was true. People were talking, but they were not really there in the room with us! That was really something! I thought that there might be little people inside, but I didn't want to press my luck by taking apart and examining the radio's guts.

We sat there and listened like little angels to the story about some hero called the Lone Ranger and his friendly Indian partner, Tonto. At the end of the thrilling tale, the Lone Ranger gave the victim he had rescued from a sad fate a silver bullet – his trademark, something to remember him by. Then, off he rode, yelling "Hi-Ho, Silver!"

Well, that was it! Those words were forever burned into my brain, and afterwards, many a stick horse was ridden off into the setting sun with me yelling, "Hi-Ho, Silver!"

Of course, *The Lone Ranger* wasn't the only program we listened to. At different times and on other days, we listened to *The Inner Sanctum* with its squeaky door, and also to *Gang Busters*, *The Shadow*, and *The Red Skelton Show*.

Actually, we did more than listen to the radio programs – we became part of their stories, living the adventures along with the radio characters. We could almost feel the wind blowing through our hair when we rode with the Lone Ranger. We could hear the guns blazing, just like we were there in the midst of it all.

Our favorite Red Skelton character was Junior, who always said, "The devil made me do it." We learned many good and bad things from Junior which we promptly tried out in our own lives. Another great Red Skelton character was Clem Kadiddlehopper, who provided many laughs to the studio's radio audience – and to us.

The roar of the crowds added to our thrill of listening to sporting events. And the colorful announcer made everything so exciting that we could just see everything in our minds, just like we were there.

Our exposure to the world of music had been fairly limited. Dad knew how to play the saxophone and violin. Occasionally, when he pulled out the violin and bow, he tried to teach us how to play. But all we got for our efforts was a shrill screech. We kids were too impatient to take the time to learn.

Instead, we listened to and played Aunt Esther's radio – that was our instrument. The radio really opened up our minds to all the kinds of music "out there." It was real special, sampling and picking out different music to learn about and just plain listen to for fun. As often as not, annoying static drowned out the music and other kinds of radio programs, but we never gave up.

Finally, our folks bought a real radio. That's when some new problems started to develop among us. Everyone wanted to tune in to different programs, so we had a lot of new arguments to work through.

The only program we could ever agree on was at Christmas time, when we all wanted to listen to *Judy, Jimmy, and the Cinnamon Bear*. What adventures they had! The program named after the three characters was a serial that ended on Christmas Eve.

We really could have used four or five radios in our house, so that everyone could listen to a different program. For us younger kids, it was hard to even find out what program options were available, because we always had to listen to the shows picked out by the oldest or biggest brother. So, we kids would sometimes split up, with some of us going up to our aunt's for some programs, and others of us staying home.

Even with the new big cabinet radio, which was about three-feet tall and thirty-plus-inches wide, the reception was so poor that we kids sat as close as possible to it. Several of us would press our ears against the speaker as the station faded away, then we'd lean back as the reception improved again. Dad finally hung up an antenna between two tall trees outside our log house and that improved our reception a bit.

Back in the late '30s, Mom and Dad liked to listen to the news. Some guy by the name of Hitler was stirring up a lot of people and everyone was talking about him. Hitler was starting a major war and that was very scary. We didn't need imagined ghosts to be scared. Of course, we couldn't listen to the radio all the time; we had work and chores to do, too. But the radio did provide our main source of "big, wide world" entertainment, and through it we discovered some new heroes.

Superman was one of our favorites. "Look – up in the air, it's a bird, it's a plane, no, it's Superman!" We tore around and roared through the house every night that show was on. Then there were Edgar Bergen, Charlie McCarthy, and Mortimer Snerd. We spent many a fun evening listening to the three of them act up and carry on.

"The radio" Our outside-world connection.

Captain Marvel, Batman and Robin also came to life in our own lives. Once, after listening to Captain Marvel, I remember standing up on the hill wearing my new little rubber boots. I thought if I ran fast enough and yelled "Shazam!" like Captain Marvel, I, too, would be able to fly. Again and again I went charging down the hill, but no matter how fast I ran, or how many times I yelled, "Shazam," I couldn't get off the ground.

I also tied a towel or dish cloth around my neck to be like Superman. That looked great, but it didn't get me off the ground, either. I couldn't understand why, if our radio heroes could fly, I couldn't fly!

-Chapter 3-
The Mouse that Roared

When I was about three years old, I became very ill. At least, I thought I was really sick. The doctor who came to our little town thought I might have appendicitis.

Although the folks had a car, for some reason I was loaded into Uncle Chuck Tandy's car and hauled to the Indian Health hospital at Nespelem, a considerable distance away. We rode for what seemed like forever, and the trip was long and dreary.

The doctor and staff at the hospital checked me over and couldn't find anything wrong. I did not like the exam they gave me one bit, so I told everybody I was better so they wouldn't examine me again. I still didn't really feel good, but the folks decided to take me home anyway. Even though many on Mom's side of the family had a history of appendix problems, they decided not to remove mine at that time.

When we headed for home, I felt a little bit better just because we were going home. I remember crossing a big river, going up a hill, then looking out of the car window at so many bright lights. The adults were talking about how so many people were working on the construction of the Grand Coulee Dam. I will always remember how all those lights lit up the night.

I spent that winter moping around the log house. A house that size can't handle a grumbly kid who can't really do much of anything except get well. Finally, I started to recover. I had been taking regularly the "cure-all" medicines of those days – cod liver oil and castor oil. I often thought that those terrible potions might do me in, if I didn't hurry up and get well.

I had a choice – to continue taking cod liver oil and castor oil or to get better. The choice was easy – I decided to get well! Taking that awful stuff was worse then dying! I can still smell and taste it. Ugh!

About the time I started feeling better, I was destroying the house by jumping on the furniture. I had to find some fun somehow. Once, I tried to leap from the couch to a metal trunk. But as I started to jump, I slipped and didn't make the distance. My head hit the trunk's sharp corner, and that really stunned me – almost knocking me out. I was aware enough to realize that blood was running down my head; then blood was everywhere. The reality of seeing my own red stuff really shocked me. I roared.

Wig, Chick and Judge wearing classic kid hats in front of the old log house. *(Photo courtesy Phoebe Wynecoop.)*

I always wondered why, when Batman was hit, he never seemed to be hurt and he never, ever, lost blood. But I felt this injury in a major way. Doctor Mom once again came to my rescue and patched up my latest wound by wrapping my head with a bandage.

That stunt-gone-wrong delayed my overall recovery for a while. But as I started feeling better, I got back to my chores again. As spring rolled around, I spent more time working and playing outside.

That winter I was sickly was a bad one for me because I didn't grow at all. And I grew very little for some time after that.

While I had been the largest baby at birth, I turned out to be the smallest adult of all of us kids. Some of my many cousins called me "Mouse," and some still do.

-Chapter 4-
Tree Games

We didn't spend all our time listening to the radio, being sick, and jumping around on furniture. While the radio had exposed us to a lot of exciting new possibilities for adventure, such as bears and bad guys, these dangers seemed far away on the radio and did not worry us as we played in our woods close to home. We had heard some mighty scary grizzly bear stories, but reportedly, there were none in our area.

For some reason, we did worry about cougars, which we thought always hung out in trees. Since we were always up in the trees, we suspected that cougars were around, too – maybe watching us. That was pretty exciting for a while. But since we had no real fierce wildlife to contend with, we came up with a new way to while away our summer days – tree climbing.

When climbing lodgepole pines, it was possible for us small, lightweight boys to swing from tree to tree. By standing on a limb high in the tree's crown and holding the bole with one hand, you could lean into another tree. Then, by grabbing the new tree's bole with your free hand, you could swing over into it.

We were light enough so that the limbs never broke, but heavy enough to tip the trees into one another. Sometimes, we felt like we were maybe half monkey. Swinging in the trees was a real free, "almost flying" feeling.

As long as we stayed in the tall thin trees, we had no trouble. We made trails through the crowns of those pine trees. Fir trees were too stiff, pitchy and thick-branched, so we avoided them.

Swinging from pine to pine was great fun, but it was a miracle that we never once fell out of a tree! Surprise!

One large fir tree had a big clump of limbs that was the perfect place for a tree house. But building it wasn't going to be easy. That tree became a real challenge – more like an impossible dream.

First, we tried to lean poles against the ball of limbs, but that didn't get us up high enough. Judge came up with the idea of throwing a rope up and over the limbs. But there was one problem with that – we weren't big enough to throw a rope that far.

Barefooted up a tree. Judge up a tree ready to swing to another tree. *(Photo courtesy Phoebe Wynecoop.)*

This particular fir tree was out in the open, so we couldn't climb a tree next to it and swing over into the clump of limbs. After considering all of the pros and cons and trying our best, we eventually gave up on the fir tree-house plan altogether.

Mom was not sure what we were doing out there in the woods, which was for the best. We knew we'd be in trouble if she ever found out about our tree play and projects.

It wasn't long before we came up with another tree game, which we called the "bucking horse." By using one pine tree that was bent over until it nearly touched the ground, and sitting on this tree and bouncing, we could make the tree "buck" up and down. We discovered that too much weight slowed the ride, so only one person at a time rode the bucking horse. The real thrill came when someone on the ground started pulling the tree up and down, or swinging the tree from side to side. Then, you had a real bucking bronco!

What a ride! You could hold onto the branches for a while, but the result was always the same – the would-be-cowboy ended up being tossed off, rolling and laughing on the ground. Up stepped the next brave rider who crawled onto the bronco, then off he galloped in a cloud of dust.

While you were hanging on for dear life with your hands, your legs just flopped around underneath, because there was nothing there for them to latch onto. The bucking horse tree could be a vicious, hard ride when a big kid made it buck. Then the rider would be toppled, fast and hard.

I could stay on as long as the tree went up and down, but sideways bucking was impossible for me. Even though the "end" result was always the same, that tree heard many a "Hi-ho, Silver!" from this cowboy.

In 1938, the twins Dick and Dave were born. They kept Mom extra busy, so we three older three boys gained more freedom. Dad was busy driving a school bus and still running our small dairy, and he had little time for us, especially during the day. When Dad was gone, working on road construction to replace roads on the Colville Reservation flooded by Grand Coulee Dam, or otherwise needed help with the dairy or ranch, he hired Louie Grinde.

When we weren't climbing trees or riding the horse tree, we wandered around in the woods, finding new fun. We pretty well covered the surrounding countryside, following old dirt roads and what was left of the logging railroad tracks. We also traced the many creeks and explored the large and small ponds. This was an interesting time in our lives. While on our explorations, we always kept a wary eye out for the imaginary cougars that continued to spook us.

By the end of summer, the bottoms of our bare feet were like leather and felt like a heavy grade of sandpaper. Yes, we always paid a price when it was time to put on shoes again. Running barefoot all summer also made our feet seem to grow wider, so our shoes always felt too tight when it was time for those attending school to get back into school clothes.

Our shoes were not in the best shape anyway. Blisters were common for us, especially when we occasionally ended up wearing one-size-fits-all hand-me-downs. With enough socks layered on, sometimes some of the shoes came close to fitting.

Wig was now a big guy, and he occasionally griped about how his shoes were too tight for his feet. Of course, he was the oldest and was, therefore, the first one to wear a pair of shoes. Once he outgrew them, if they were

**The "Dead End Gang" front to back: Steve (1), Wig (2), Judge (3),
Chick (4), Dick (5), Dave (6) and Louie Grinde (7).** *(Wynecoop photo)*

still wearable, Judge was next in line. I was next in line, if there was any thing left of them to wear. Wearing my older brothers' shoes was kind of special. They were well broken in by the time they got to me, comfortable, and meant I had grown.

Being the oldest, Wig was the first one of us kids to take on the school adventure. Once Wig started school, he thought he was pretty hot stuff. Man, the stories he told made us want to go, too, just as soon as we could. We really envied him. But we were too young, so we just waited for him to come home in the afternoon.

Every day after school, Wig brought home his school papers and we got ready to do our lessons. Wig made us sit down and then he would show us what he had done in school. Judge and I practiced our ABC's, tried a little reading, and did a lot of coloring. When our times finally came, we were ready for school – thanks to Wig's early version of home-school and kindergarten.

Dave, Dick and Tim were the keys to freedom at the log house. *(Photo courtesy Phoebe Wynecoop)*

Wig, the well-dressed school kid in the 1930s. (*Photo courtesy Phoebe Wynecoop)*

Judge and Chick forcing Dick to pose for the camera. *(Photo courtesy Phoebe Wynecoop)*

-Chapter 5-
Chores Galore

Dad's dairy provided a work outlet for our boundless energy, but there were certain rules we had to follow. We weren't supposed to go out to the barn alone. With adult supervision, we were allowed to turn the handle to the separator to separate the cream from the milk. This device sent the milk into one container and cream into another. We used cream for making butter or enjoyed it just by itself as a topping on fruits or cereal. "Separating" was one of our first childhood chores.

The old separator was pretty tough to manage, especially since the handle was head-high for us kids. Usually, we stood up on a block of wood or a chair, then tried to turn the handle. We met with some success, but Mom or Dad eventually had to finish the job. Afterwards, we got to wash the separator, or at least rinse it off and carry the parts to the wash pan. We did get some sense of accomplishment for our efforts.

That chore ranked right up there with carrying wood and water. Dad cut the wood and I carried it to the wood box and kept it full for Mom to use for cooking, for heating water, and for heating the house.

Of course, these chores really opened our eyes to a whole new world of work out there. And there was much more to do than house chores. As I mentioned, we were living on a small ranch dairy farm stocked with real horses, bulls, cows, pigs, and barnyards, barns and hay. Caring for the livestock took a lot of work – cutting and hauling hay, feeding and tending the animals.

We learned that at some future time we would be expected to do our share of the other work and we looked forward to that day. There was no question about our doing the work! The only question that ever came up was when we could we do our share of the work.

We gave the livestock a lot of room. To us kids, the cows were giants, and the horses were huge, and both were dangerous. Even though we were not big enough to take on the job of working with the animals, we were able to carry wood and water.

The water buckets were too heavy for us, but we wanted to help, so the folks let us try. The large bucket was almost as tall as I was at five years old, especially when the handle was up.

Even though we probably caused more problems than we helped solve, Dad taught us to never stand around and watch someone work. So, we joined in the best we could. Dad was seldom critical of our work habits. We were more subject to punishment if we stood around than if we tried to do something and couldn't do it well or at all.

Judge, Chick and Wig, dressed for winter chores with their "bomber caps." *(Photo courtesy Phoebe Wynecoop)*

There were some smaller buckets for us kids to use. But even small buckets full of water seemed very heavy to us. Each Christmas, we found a new bunch of small buckets under the tree filled with hard candy, ribbon candy and sometimes even chocolates. After eating the sweets, we had a new supply of work buckets that were just our size. My folks always made sure our presents were practical in the long run.

With five boys and our parents now living in the little old log house, water was always in high demand. The well was down at the bottom of a monster of a hill. At least, that is what it seemed like to a four or five year old.

The water pump had a small metal hump on top of the spout. First, I hung the handle of the bucket behind the hump. Then, I worked the adult-sized handle up and down until, eventually, water poured out the mouth into the bucket. Once the bucket was full, I had to lift it over the hump, then off the pump. This was really hard, because the pump was about 18 inches high. Once I got the bucket off, the real work started – lugging it back up the steep hill.

Judge and I soon realized that one of us could not carry the bucket alone without spilling half of the water during the climb. So, we devised a plan to make the water hauling easier, with each of us grabbing one side of the handle. As long as we were fresh, we could do okay; but as we tired, which didn't take very long, the taller person's side of the bucket was naturally higher. I was the shorter one, so there was many an argument about how Judge would purposely raise his side of the bucket so that I'd get wet. I'd scream and yell at him to stop spilling the water on my pants and feet. I also was known to use a few colorful words that I had heard other people use. My vocabulary was starting to expand, but not in the best direction.

Of course, as the water spilled out, the bucket became lighter and easier to carry. We quickly figured out that it was better to start out with a half-full bucket than to tote a full bucket. This way I didn't get so wet, and we still got the same amount of water up the hill. You could say we learned some lessons along the way.

Sometimes, getting water up to the house was the least of our worries. Winter presented new wrinkles in an already difficult situation. No matter what kind of weather hit, we still hauled water.

When it was really cold, the pump occasionally froze, so Dad would start a fire around the pump to thaw it out. But in the winter when we spilled water on the hill, it turned into solid ice from top to bottom. As we slipped and slid, we went down many times, spilling the whole bucket of water. Four-lettered words echoed down the hill from both of our young mouths.

One time, when we were at the pump, I slipped on the ice, landed on the ground, and hit my head on a stick of firewood we had carried for a fire to thaw the pump. Once again, something was running down the side

Winter problems. *(Photo courtesy Ruth Hintze)*

of my face and forehead. It was red, red blood, and I knew I must be mortally wounded. I started screaming and yelling, and the folks came sliding down the hill to rescue me. Dad helped me up the hill and Mom patched me up.

In those days, doctors were far away, so we were usually patched up by the folks and sent on our way. We only went to a doctor for a major injury, not for minor injuries or for most of our health problems.

This time, with my special luck, I'd landed right on the same place that I'd hit when jumping to the trunk. It seemed like my head had just barely healed from the trunk accident when it was called into battle again. I was becoming much too familiar with head cuts.

However, there was a fun side to the water pump and the monster hill in the wintertime. When icicles froze at the mouth of the pump, we'd lick them or sometimes break them off and chew on them. Of course, it got dangerous if you got too close to the metal. If your tongue touched the metal on the pump, you were stuck tight, hanging from it by your tongue.

This was a real problem with a couple of possible solutions. You could wait for your tongue to warm the pump, or you could pour water on your tongue and the pump. You soon learned what not to do. You'd never try to pull your tongue off or you'd painfully lose a chunk of skin. We all learned fast about the strange connection between warm tongues and cold metal.

In later years, we passed on our vast knowledge by luring a few victims into licking something metal and frozen, knowing full well what the results would be. Sometimes, our naughty selves won out over our angel selves and we led a few innocent kids right to trouble.

Carrying water on wash day was the hardest job of all. I am sure that Mom, Dad and Wig carried most of the water, even though Judge and I thought we did the biggest part of the work. One way or another, Mom had enough water to wash all of our clothes.

We also tried to help with the clothes washing, especially once Dad bought a washing machine. I usually enjoyed helping Mom with this chore. She filled the tub with hand-hauled water, then added the soap and loaded in the dirty clothes. The washer gurgled and sloshed until the clothes were clean. Then she put the clothes through the wringer. That bordered on being dangerous, because it was easy to get your hand caught in the wringer. Under the wringer was a small tray that caught the water and drained it back into the tub. If, for some unknown rascal reason I wanted to make Mom mad, I'd reach up and tilt the tray the other way. Then the water would run on to the floor. That was bad news, and running away from Mom as fast as I could was my only option. But I was always caught and then I had to mop up the mess.

Once the clothes were run through the wringer, Mom took the still wet, heavy wash outside and hung it on the clothesline to dry. Sun-and-wind-dried clothes dried stiff, but that was okay with us, because that's what we were used to.

Before we got the electric washing machine, Mom used a washboard to scrub our dirty clothes. The old washboard was hard on the hands and fingers, and we younger kids were not strong enough to use it, so Mom had to do all the washing, especially toiling over our soiled pants and diapers.

Wig and Judge were a lot more helpful than I was about most things. Judge always said that since he was older, he should get to do things first. He was bigger than I was and always bugged me, so I told him that some day I was going to be older and then I'd get to do things first.

Carrying wood was a lot easier than hauling water. Our system for that chore was simple. You picked up as much wood as you could carry, took it into the house, put it in the wood box and then went back for more.

Even though we wanted to try to cut some of the wood, we weren't allowed to do that. The old ax was big and sharp, so our wood chores were limited to carrying and stacking what Dad cut. We occasionally sneaked in a chop or two, but that was it.

With a wood kitchen stove and another heating stove, we always used a lot of wood. The kitchen stove needed small kindling for starting the fire and split wood two or three inches thick by 15 to 18 inches long. The heating stove burned much larger pieces of wood. Just as soon as wood pieces were split, we carried them to dry by the kitchen stove. Wood for the kitchen stove had to be well seasoned and dry, because green wood would not burn in it. Each stove had its own stack of wood piled high beside it, always ready for use.

-Chapter 6-
Playing Outside

Like most kids, we fussed about doing chores, but they didn't ever last long, then we headed back to the old dirt pile for some fun. We didn't have many toys to play with, but as far as we knew, no better toys existed. Sticks and short pieces of a board were good enough toys for us. We

could dig the soil with a stick and smooth it over again, using a board for a bulldozer. We made car and tractor noises for added special effects. We built roads like we knew what we were doing. We probably looked like a bunch of dirty pigs when the fun was done at the end of the day.

Once, the three of us were out rooting around in the dirt when our cousin Larry rode his bike into our dirt pile. Max our ever-faithful Collie watchdog and companion, growled, then bit Larry on the leg. We thought Max was right in biting Larry. Our loyal dog was just protecting us from an intruder on a bike.

Max, our guardian and friend, with Chick, Wig, and Judge. *(Photo courtesy Phoebe Wynecoop)*

Again, Mom came to rescue the wounded party, bandaged him up and sent him home. A day or so later, a stranger came to our house and talked to the folks. Then he took Max away. Back then, everyone was afraid of rabies, and they worried about Max because of past rabies epidemics. Supposedly, they took Max away to check him for rabies. That sounded okay to us. We just wanted to know when Max would be coming home.

We never saw Max again. We heard that he'd died from the test. We didn't realize that the test required his death, so they could check his brain. When we found out later what had happened, we were really shocked that someone would kill the world's greatest dog. Max had been our playmate and friend. It was a sad day when we found out that Max would not ever come home.

Dad missed Max, too. He'd trained that dog to chase the cows home. Dad would name a cow and send Max out to bring her in for milking. Max would go find that particular cow and bring her into the barn. Losing Max was sorely felt by all of us. We three older boys always thought that the authorities had checked the wrong participant of the accident for being crazy. Larry was the one who had crashed his bike into where we were playing. Max was just doing his job and protecting us. Sometimes the rules of life are hard to figure out.

That wasn't the only dirt pile we had. Up and across the road near the "bucking horse" tree, we found another with some loose, soft dirt at the bottom of a bank. We found we could easily dig a hole into the cut bank. What a discovery! Gathering several tin cans and a couple pieces of steel which were stronger for digging than sticks, we started our excavation.

We planned to use our hole as a hiding place. Of course, like everything else we did, we got a little carried away, and pretty soon we had two holes. Then we connected them in the back until we had made a short tunnel. What a big deal! We'd made our own tunnel. Judge and I worked especially hard digging it, and we were really proud of our final creation. We ran home to tell Mom. She got one of those looks on her face that meant trouble. She could tell by looking at our clothes that we had been digging deep. Right away, she asked to see our prized tunnel. When she got there, the orders flew fast and furious. The big kids were ordered to cave in the tunnel – she didn't care how. Using a shovel, it didn't take long for them to demolish our fantastic project. That ended our dirt tunnel fun. We never even thought about how the tunnel might cave in on us. Hidden dangers never entered our minds. The digging had been fun and easy, pure and simple. We didn't know enough to be scared about the possibility of cave-ins and then our suffocation.

-Chapter 7-
Adventures-A-Plenty

About that same time, we found a hatchet on a shelf behind the ax near the wood pile. We knew better than to touch the ax, but the hatchet was different and the rules hadn't been handed down on using it. We should have known that the ax rules still applied, but what a neat little hatchet it was.

After some arguing, Judge claimed that he was now, by all rights, the oldest since Wig was off to school. That qualified him as the proud possessor of the hatchet. Up the hill we went to attack a small tree that he wanted to chop down. First, he cut off some of the limbs, so they wouldn't be in his way or slow down his swing.

Then Judge started to cut the tree trunk. But a five or six year old couldn't hit very hard, and the chips were not flying. So I thought that if I got the chips out of the cut, he would be able to cut faster. But Judge wouldn't stop cutting to let me do my part and clean out the chips. I kept telling him to stop, but like all bigger and wiser older brothers, he said, "No, just get your finger out of the way, or I will cut it."

I still thought that the chips were in his way. But talking sense into him was like talking to the tree – he just would not stop hacking. Stubbornly, I sneaked a couple of quick scrapes in between his chops, but I wasn't very effective.

"Once more," I yelled as I poked my finger into the wood cut – and he hit it! Whack! "Yeeow!" I yelped. I couldn't believe that he had actually hit me with the hatchet. That really hurt! I was surprised that he'd been able to hit the same place twice. And I was hurting from both the actual hit and the realization that he would chop me up. He almost cut off the end of my finger – the tip was just hanging over to the side. I ran down the hill to Nurse Mom. She cleaned out the bloody gash, and bandaged my finger back together with just gauze and tape – no stitches, no glue. The cut eventually healed and my finger was okay, but I still have a scar from that ax bite. I am sure Mom punished Judge. We also knew Dad would be the main one to punish us.

When Dad came home he gave us a real chewing out about the hatchet and how dangerous it was in small kids' hands. He said, "I had that hatchet hid from you guys and you should have known better! Especially you, Judge! You're older and I expect you to show some responsibility." I'd rather have had a spanking than a scolding. Of course, I whole- heartedly agreed, since my finger was the one that had been almost cut off. Judge had been the real "hatchet man."

By now, I was starting to collect a few scars which were the by-product of country living with two older brothers who claimed to be wiser than me. More than once, I suffered the consequences of my total trust in them as my leaders. I followed them around blindly doing lots of dumb things.

One time, I was out in the barnyard wearing my warm bomber hat and heavy coat. Dad had ordered us kids to stay out of that dangerous place, but I was there anyway. Why? To watch Dad and Wig milk the cows, and to play in the hay, of course.

I had made it halfway across the barnyard, sloshing through the mud and cow manure, when "thump" – down I went into the mire. I was stunned and not quite sure what had happened. The shock quickly wore off when I had a face full of hair – cow hair! A full-grown cow had knocked me down and had her heavy head against my chest and stomach.

I tried to get up, but she pinned me on my back. Her horns were stuck in the cold ground on each side of me. There was no way I could escape. It was a good thing that I was small and that her horns couldn't penetrate the partially-frozen ground, because she couldn't crush me. All she could do was hold me down and push me around in the mud and manure.

I still thought I was going to be crushed to death or maybe even drown. My coat was wet and got even heavier. My arms were pinned so they were useless. That cow never raised her head. She probably thought that since she had me down good, she was just going to keep me there forever. The more she pushed me around the barnyard, the louder I screamed.

It seemed a lifetime had passed, and then I heard one loud *whomp*! and then another. By then, I was pretty much out of it and didn't know what was going on. All I knew was that she lifted up her head and I heard another noise. There was Dad, kicking the cow. She ran off a ways, so Dad picked me up and scraped the mud and cow manure off me. Dad was really puffing and kind of shaking. Once we both settled down a bit, he asked me if I wanted to kick the cow, too.

I was trying to understand what had happened, wondering if I was still alive, but it sounded like a good idea and I was all for it. So Dad grabbed me by the arms from behind and away we went, chasing that cow around the barnyard – and kicking her at every step or two. Dad would kick her and I would swing at her, and what a time we had!

We still don't know why that particular cow attacked me. She had never been mean before. But she could have killed me. All she had to do was raise her head and poke me with one of her horns and I would have been a goner.

I knew Dad was really mad at me for violating one of his rules. I didn't know if he was going to spank me or just chew on me for awhile. I did learn a few more cuss words while we were kicking the cow.

Once was enough for me to learn this lesson. I knew I was lucky to be alive. After that, I stayed away from the barnyard for a long time when the cows were there – probably for two whole days.

A suspect in the field. *(Wynecoop photo)*

-Chapter 8-
Hay Play

While the cows were down in the field, we were allowed to go into the barn and play in the hay. This was one of our favorite winter games. Jumping from one of the rafters, I felt that I could fly like a bird before "landing" on the cushion of hay below. We even practiced our diving and did flips in the air, always landing safely in the soft hay. We'd go at it until we were completely played out – it was great fun for us kids.

When the barn was full of hay, we'd work our way across the barn under the beams that held the structure together. There was also a board on top of the rafters that ran down the middle of the barn. We liked to burrow under the board and rafters. This gave us a network of hay tunnels in the top of the barn. We spent many hours playing in these tunnels that would not cave in like our dirt tunnel might have.

I got smart and figured out a way of going up the hill to get to the barn without having to go near the cows. Once inside the barn, I crawled up into the hay. Then, using either a pitch fork or my hands, I pushed the hay down to the manger for the cows to eat.

While the cows were eating, Dad and Wig milked them by hand. Once in a while we kids crawled down to watch them milk. If we were lucky, they squirted milk towards us and we tried to catch it in our open mouths. They usually missed, and milk hit us everywhere else, but it was a lot of fun. Body temperature milk is not that tasty, but the cats really liked getting it that way.

We also were strongly encouraged to go into the empty barn and help clean it of smelly manure and dirty hay. That was a nasty job, but we helped, once in a while.

As you can imagine, the hay that we fed to the cows didn't get there by itself. Dad cut and hauled it from a small field below the house. We were too small to help him with that chore, so Dad borrowed a team of horses or someone would come and help him move the hay. We could follow him around, but that got old and boring fast, and we usually went home before long.

I've already mentioned that Dad had bought some land a mile or two away where he planned to build a big house. Summers, we followed Dad down to this land that we called "The Ranch," to help him with the hay. Like everything else, we caused more problems than we helped solve. Of course, Dad knew that some day we would be able to help, and he didn't want to dampen our spirits.

Dad had made a tractor out of an old truck, and he pulled the mower and hay rake with this old vehicle. Occasionally, he drove the tractor to and from the ranch. We kids thought it was neat to catch a ride on the tractor. But for safety's sake, when he was pulling the mower or rake, we weren't allowed to ride on the back.

Once the hay was raked and dried it was shocked into piles. Then Dad got a wagon and, using a pitch fork, threw the hay up onto the wagon. That was hard work. A lot of the hay would fall off the fork and end up all over you. If the day was warm, the hay dust stuck to your skin. Wild hay really smelled good, but the itching and scratching that came with it was a real pain.

We kids couldn't throw the hay onto the wagon, because the bed was too high. It would take all day for us to pile in one load. When Dad started throwing the hay onto the wagon, we crawled into the hay and moved it around enough so he could put on a good load. After the wagon was more than full, Dad pulled the load of hay up to the barn and threw it in.

I don't remember if we had our own team of work horses, so I guess Dad borrowed them when he needed to. The heavy harnesses were made to fit the huge horses. Actually, we had fun riding in the hay-filled wagon or sled all year long. Sometimes, we got to ride in a hay sleigh pulled by a team of horses. We burrowed down deep into the hay to stay warm. I remember how snow flew from the horses' hooves as they trotted along.

If we were riding in an empty sleigh, we had no protection from the wind as we moved along, so we tried to play to keep warm. One of our games was to try to see who could stand up the longest without holding on while the horses moved along. It was hard to keep standing for long in the middle of a bouncing, swaying sleigh or wagon.

The hay we gathered was mostly wild hay, but each year Dad planted a field of oats. He used a combine that made bundles of oats that were stacked into what, I believe, were called shocks. When dried, the shocks were hauled up to the hay barn. Oat bundles had to be stacked in a special manner. The stem was to the outside and the top of the stalk was put in the center. This way, the better part the grain was kept out of the weather.

Oats were a valuable crop, important both for their grain and for straw. We couldn't play in the oat stacks part of the barn, because we might have knocked off the precious oat grains. The cats really liked the oats, because the mice were after the oats and the cats were after the mice...and so it went.

Uncle Chuck Tandy's homemade tractor. *(Photo courtesy Dot Tandy)*

-Chapter 9-
First Smokes

We had heard that oat straws were supposed to be good to smoke, so we logged that in our brains. One day when we were in the upper barnyard, someone suggested that we try smoking an oat straw. Dad smoked, but Mom didn't. So we thought "Let's be like Dad and give smoking a try." We did.

We found some oat straw, then carefully selecting the larger part of the straw, we proceeded to light up. Like real smokers, we took a big drag. Wow! Talk about hot! It was like trying to smoke a flame-thrower. Since the straw was hollow, the burning smoke came right up the hollow core when you sucked on it. If you waited for the fire to get smaller, it would go out, so you had to start puffing right from the time it was first lit.

Next we tried smoking longer straws, but you had to do a lot of sucking to keep them burning. Once they started blazing, the heat still came right up the core. That was no good either. The smoke was so hot that we thought that we had burned our mouths, but they were only singed, not burned.

Oat smoke was also hard on the eyes; Tears welled up, then ran down our cheeks leaving mud trails. When Mom asked what we had been doing, we said, "Playing outside." But our muddy cheeks must have been dead giveaways as to what we'd really been up to.

Since dad was a heavy smoker, he bought a machine that he could use for rolling his own cigarettes. We boys quickly took over the job for him because it looked like fun. We would be kind enough to roll him a bunch of cigarettes at a time.

After our episode with the oat straw, we decided to sneak a couple of the cigarettes we made for him. To the barnyard we went, to fire up the real McCoys. Once we had them burning, we sat back like real smokers and took long, slow drags on our first cigarettes.

Then we started coughing and choking. Our eyes watered, and we rubbed them so hard they turned red. And we smelled. Cigarette smoke has a way of staying with you; even your clothes stink. Mom didn't have to be much of a detective to figure out that we'd been smoking.

Prior to Dad's buying the cigarette rolling machine, he'd rolled his own. A person who had perfected the art of rolling cigarettes could do it one-handed. Dad was one of those folks who could fold and crease the paper with three fingers, then pour the tobacco into the creased paper, then fold it over, then roll the paper and tobacco into a nice looking cigarette – all with one hand. Once it was rolled, he licked the paper on the seam, twisted the ends, and he had it – the perfect hand-rolled cigarette.

We thought paper, any paper would do, so first we tried rolling newspaper cigarettes. We carefully tore a square piece, poured on the tobacco, rolled it up nice and tight, then lit it. Wow! We got more than we expected! The fire was big and fast, the tobacco fell on the ground, and we were lucky to still have our eyebrows after the smoke cleared.

Dad made it look easy, so under his supervision, we had to give that a try, too. For us kids, the one-handed technique was out of the question. We double-handed it. First we creased the paper (real cigarette paper was thin and soft) which made it stiff enough so that we could grip it. Then with the other steady hand, we poured a generous supply of tobacco onto the paper. Of course, most of the time, the paper would bend and spill the tobacco. It seemed like we needed more hands – or at least a helper. That way one of us could use two hands to hold the paper while someone else poured the tobacco onto it.

We finally got hold of some real cigarette paper. We carefully poured on the tobacco, then rolled the paper. You had to be sure to pour the tobacco on the outer one-third of the paper to allow for more paper to cover the tobacco. Once you started to roll the cigarette, you had to hold it flat. If you didn't, the tobacco dribbled out the end. Once the cigarette was rolled, just like the big guys, you'd lick down the seam and twist the ends and you were in business.

Most of the time, the paper didn't stick together and the cigarette ruptured in the middle, or the ends were not twisted right, or the paper was too dry and the paper burned up like our newspaper cigarettes, or we didn't put in enough tobacco – something usually went wrong.

Lighting up required more specialized talent. If you wanted to do it right, cowboy style, you had to light the match on the seat of your pants. To do that, you put the match on the lower part of or just below your hip pocket. Then you'd rub it a little to warm it up. Then you'd rip it across your pants – and the friction caused the match to light.

To light a match that way, your pants had to be really tight. If you raised your leg, your pants tightened up even more, thus improving your chance of lighting the match. With some luck there was ignition. Most often, we broke the match or jerked so hard that the tobacco fell out of the prized hand-rolled cigarette. We spent a lot of time ripping matches across our hind ends trying to just light the match, let alone getting around to lighting the cigarette.

Sometimes the match would light! But you were so used to repeating the process that you automatically ripped it across again, leaving a brown strip across your pants.

Not any old pants would light a match. Levis were the only pants for us. Essentially, any pair of jeans would work, but Levis were the best.

Our ultimate goal was to light a cigarette, sit back and blow smoke rings. Dad and Granddad did that, so that was what we tried to copy. But after our pitiful efforts, our eyes were usually tearing so bad that we couldn't have seen a smoke ring even if we had ever managed to blow one. We knew this much – that when you smoke cigarettes, you smell like what you smoke. We had also learned that chewing pine needles helps to clean up smoker's breath. While that may have been true, the pine needles didn't do anything for the rest of your body and clothes. We chewed on so many pine needles, the tree looked like it was diseased or dying.

We also knew that to be real smokers, we had to blow smoke through our noses. Of course, all that did was singe our noses and start up all that choking and coughing again. Man, smoking was fun! We darn near died from our early cigarette experiments!

After our first feeble efforts, we laid off smoking for a while. But I can remember another experience when we were lying on the bank above the road and decided to smoke some dead grass. That was terrible ... awful ... just like our other smoking adventures.

Most of our crazy smoking ideas had come from older cousins or friends. Because they were older, we listened to them. That was true for both the good and bad ideas. We had been taught to listen to and obey older adults and even older kids.

We also tried mullein weed. Mullein gets to be very tall and has large green fuzzy leaves. Somewhere we had heard that the old Indians smoked them as cigars by drying the leaves, then rolling them.

We didn't take the time to dry the leaves. We just picked off the lower leaves that were already a little dry. We didn't have any cigarette paper, so we wrapped the crumpled leaves in newspaper. Since Judge was older, he got to try our first mullein cigarette.

The newspaper burned so fast, it was hard for Judge to figure out if mullein was any good for smoking. Once the newspaper started burning, the flame was so big it burned part of Judge's eyebrows and some of his hair, too.

 After watching Judge's bonfire I decided not to try the same thing without modifying the process. I figured that if I crushed up the mullein leaves to look like tobacco and twisted the newspaper tighter after licking and sealing it, it would work. My cigarette burned a little slower, but it flamed way too fast to consider it true smoking.

Knowing how to use the Bull Durham sack of tobacco was also an important part of cigarette rolling. Attached to the top of the bag of tobacco was a drawstring with a paper circle on the end of it. If you were really cool, you held the bag in one hand, rolled the cigarette with the other hand, and bit the paper and pulled the bag closed with your teeth. That was the master roller's way to do it. We never in our wildest dreams approached this level of skill.

Tobacco also came in a metal can, courtesy of Prince Albert. The empty can was the real treasure, because you could keep lots of important things in it. For example, it was considered to be the best thing there was to keep your fishing worms in and it was just the right size to fit into a pants or shirt pocket. When that Prince Albert can was filled with angleworms, you knew you were ready to go fishing.

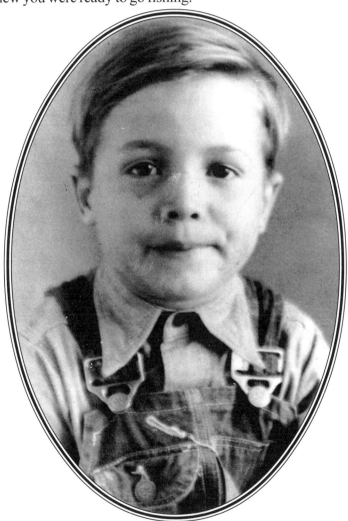

Judge, the youthful-looking juvenile smoker.

-Chapter 10-
Grandparents

Once in a while, we'd walk a half mile to Grandma and Granddad Galbraith's place. To get there, we had to take the main road, which had very little traffic. We had been taught to give all cars a lot of room. But if a rare car passed us, we were more surprised than scared of it.

Granddad worked for the government and lived in a house at the Agency. His yard was full of flowers and was such a pretty place. Granddad, like everyone else living at the Agency at Wellpinit, took great pride in his yard.

Mom and Dad were both from large families, and many of their brothers and sisters lived close by. Many of Mom's brothers and sisters were in high school or were away at college, so we didn't see them very often. But when we did get together with our aunts and uncles on Mom's side of the family, we had a lot of fun.

Mom's parents, Bill and May (Etue) Galbraith. *(Photo courtesy Ruth Hintze)*

Dad's brothers and sisters were all older and had their own families, so we didn't get together with them very often. When we did see their kids, they usually got us into trouble – they were the older cousins I referred to.

Mom's parents' house was so big and fun to play in. Grandma always had little snacks and a lot of magazines for us to "picture read," including a large collection of *National Geographic* magazines. What a treasure those were – with pictures of far away places and people from different countries. Those magazines helped us see outside of our Reservation world.

They also had a stereo-viewer that was awesome. Since the viewer's pictures had depth like 3-D, they just came alive. They had 3-D pictures from Egypt, pictures of the pyramids, the Nile River, large Egyptian cities, animals, etc. Granddad was tall – over six feet – and always smoked a big cigar. He kept his smokes in a round, brownish-yellow plastic type container that kept the cigars from drying out. Whenever I think of Granddad, I remember the nice cigar smell that usually surrounded him. Grandma was small, only about five-feet tall, and an odd match, size-wise.

Now I want to take you back to Granddad Galbraith's yard and garden. They were really something to see. Big trees grew in front of and on the side of the house. The grass was always green, soft and cool. The lawn was cut with a hand push lawnmower. I tried to push that mower several times, but it was too big for me.

Behind the house was Granddad's vegetable garden. It seemed like everything in it grew so well. He grew carrots, onions, corn, potatoes, squash, beets, etc.

L. to R.: Cousin Lorena Knoll, Wig and Judge in Granddad's garden. *(Wynecoop photo)*

Granddad also had a large flower garden near the back of his house. You could tell he really enjoyed making things grow.

Granddad was always outside working in one of his gardens, or in the yard, smoking one of his cigars.

Mom tried to grow a garden at our place, but it needed to be irrigated. As I previously noted, we had to carry all the water up to the house, so her garden was not watered very often.

Next to Granddad's garden was a building with a woodshed on one end and a garage at the other. Just off the garage end of the shed was a small gate through which a trail ran from the school to the store. That trail cut through the Agency square, past the office, clinic and jail, up and over a hill and across the road to the store. All the kids used that trail, since the post office was also inside of the store.

While visiting at my grandparents' house before I was old enough to go to school, I could see the school and all of the kids playing outside. I couldn't wait until I was old enough to go to school.

I traveled that trail many times, once I started to go to school. And someone always had to pick up the mail. That was a daily job. In those days, you'd get real important mail – not all the flyers and junk of today.

When I found out that the folks had a store account which they paid off each month, I decided I would buy myself a candy bar every time I picked up the mail. Mom found out at the end of the first month, and that ended my candy bar reward for getting the mail. She was not very happy about the bill I had run up. That candy along with other sweets caused me to pay dearly in other ways, because later, cavities in my teeth became a problem.

We went to our Grandparents' place during Thanksgiving and Christmas for dinner and presents. At these big family gatherings, all of the little ones had to eat at the kitchen table. We couldn't wait until we were big enough to eat at the dining room table with the adults.

When dinner time rolled around, all of us kids would stand around dreading

Sent to the porch after a big meal. Left to right: Steve (in hat), Judge (behind Steve), Dick, Dave, unknown, Wig, and Tim (the dog) in front and Tex behind Wig. *(Photo courtesy Ruth Hintze)*

Dad's parents, John and Nancy Wynecoop. *(Wynecoop photo)*

being assigned to the kitchen table. We ate the same food as was served at the dining room table, but we wanted more than anything to listen to the adults talk. Since there was no room for us at the adults' table, we had to wait for an opening. We also had to grow tall enough to reach the top of the table before we could join the adults.

While they were laughing and carrying on in the dining room, we tried our best to hear what they were talking about. After a while, we just resigned ourselves to our fate, and visited with our cousins: Squeak, Midge, Ken and Gene. Since we were the largest family there, my brothers and I pretty well dominated the kitchen table conversation.

When we were around relatives during the holidays or when they came to visit us, we always had to put up with the dreaded "Kissing Aunts," especially one particular aunt on Dad's side of the family. The usual game was: "Oh, there is little Bobby! I want to give him a big kiss and a hug." Those words were enough to put the fear of God in me.

Dad's sister Bernice was the worst aunt for kissing and hugging. Aunt Bernice had two older boys, Dale and Curtis, that we actually enjoyed visiting and playing with. If I remember anything about growing up, it will be Aunt Bernice reaching for me, grabbing me and giving me a big kiss and a hug. She was a large lady and she would almost smother me with her hugs.

Bernice's demonstrations of affection have now become a family thing. I once made the mistake of telling my kids about the cheek pinching, and now they pinch my cheek while in a falsetto voice they tease, "There's little Bobby! My, how you have grown."

-Chapter 11-
Clothes for the Day and Beds for the Night

Mom tried to dress us in our best to go to the holiday dinners, but after running barefoot all summer, we had a hard time fitting our feet into shoes. Dressing up meant putting on our best pair of bibbed overalls, a light-colored button-down-the-front shirt, shoes and socks. We always wore bibbed overalls, because Dad said we had snake hips that wouldn't hold up our pants. We could wear suspenders, but they usually came unsnapped and Dad was right. When they did our pants fell down.

Mom wanted us to wear shorts during the summer, but we had heard that only sissies wore shorts, and no way would we be caught dead in shorts. We never figured out that there would be less water to carry because of fewer clothes to wash if we'd suited up in shorts. But no way would we be considered sissies! Our pride was more important than practicality!

On my fourth or fifth birthday, Mom told me to go down to her parents' house because Grandma had something for me. So after I got cleaned up, down the road I went – along the main road, then down the road towards the school, and then up the trail to their house.

Dapper dresser Wig in shorts and Mica socks
(Wynecoop photo)

When I got there, Grandma offered me some cookies and milk, as usual. Then she gave me a present – a yellow sweatshirt. What a present! To me, that long-sleeved yellow sweatshirt appeared magical. I remember strutting home wearing it. Man, was I proud of that sweatshirt! I wore that sweatshirt until it was a rag.

Mom's brother, my uncle Glenn, had said I could have one of his old hats. It was tan with a yellow *"I"* on the front. Glenn was going to college at the University of Idaho, therefore the *"I"*. I really thought it was pretty neat,

Dick, Dave, Steve and Wig, dressed for dinner. *(Wynecoop photo)*

because my new hat looked like a sailor hat. With the side of the hat folded up, the *"I"* showed; if the rim was folded down, the *"I"* didn't show. All the adults wore hats and we kids were starting to wear them, so when I wore Uncle Glenn's hat, I fit right in with the older folks.

Kid's hats were usually different from regular adult hats. We'd take an old adult hat and cut the top out of it and bend up the sides, and then we had what we called a skull cap. We also cut little teeth around the outer edge, then folded it up one to two inches. That made a real neat kids' hat that sat on the back of our head. The cartoon character Jughead had made that style famous.

You could also take the cork out of a pop bottle cap, and then put the cap on the outside of the hat brim, and then squeeze the cork and hat back into the bottle cap until they stayed stuck together. These bottle caps decorated our hats and made them special. The resulting hats were pretty small, and would only fit on the backs of our heads, but that was fine with us.

Chick wearing a winter knit cap. *(Photo by Phoebe Wynecoop)*

-Chapter 12-
Dick Is Lost

One day I was out behind the house doing little to nothing when Mom asked me if I would help her. She said my little brother Dick was in her way and asked if I'd watch him for a while. That sounded simple enough, but watching a little brother was about the last thing I wanted to do. Dick and his orange-striped cat, Red Wing, came outside to join me.

As usual, I wandered off to do something and forgot about Dick.It wasn't long before Mom came out to see how we were doing. "Where's Dick?" she asked. After we quickly looked around, it was obvious that Dick was missing. He had slipped away, and I didn't have any idea where he'd gone. I felt terrible, because I hadn't done my job. Mom and I started looking for him, and soon other people joined in.

I don't know who found him, but he was spotted a couple of hours later on a log in a pond. He wasn't really feeling lost. He had just been tracking old Red Wing, who had been out on one of his regular hunting trips.

Dick with Redwing, the cat, in 1941. *(Photo courtesy Phoebe Wynecoop)*

We had all been to that pond several times on our own explorations, and had thrown sticks and rocks into it, to see the water splash. But when Dick disappeared, we never thought of looking for him there.

When we found him, Dick's feet were wet and muddy, but since he was barefooted, that didn't matter. Unlike us, he was not a bit concerned. Dick knew exactly where he was.

Naturally, Mom and Dad were not too happy with me. After we all got home, they chewed on me for a while. I preferred a spanking to being chewed on, because a chewing-out lasted longer. And once your guilty conscience got involved, it could take a long, long time to get over.

Sweet and innocent Dick at Grandparents' house. *(Wynecoop photo)*

-Chapter 13-
Bucked Off

Sometimes Dad would say, "Okay, boys, let's go down to the ranch." That was usually a welcome invitation, but not always. We'd oblige and follow Dad when he asked us. We always went with him when he drove his tractor, which was fun to ride. At other times we walked.

It was about a mile from our house to the ranch, and after working for several hours, I got tired, especially if I had to walk home.

Once when I was really tired, I was lagging way behind everybody else. We still had a long way to go, and I was wondering if I could make it home. After passing through a gate leaving our land, the trail went through our neighbor, Mose Phillips', yard. We often stopped to get a drink from the pipe feeding their water trough. Our neighbor Mose was a local politician, and Dad liked to visit with him.

Seeing I was so far behind, Dad picked me up and put me on Cricket, our saddle horse he was leading. Cricket was a high-strung horse that pranced around and shied away from the slightest movement. I was glad to be riding in Cricket's saddle, with Dad holding the reins and walking in front with Wig and Judge. I held onto the saddle horn, and was just nonchalantly riding along – but not for long.

Well, this time things did not work well out at Mose's place. Suddenly, Cricket put his head down and bucked and kicked up his back legs. As he brought his hind end up, he threw me high in the air. I came down, landing head-first on a board, that cut a long gash down the top of my head. The shock and realization that I had been bucked off caught us all by surprise.

I was screaming and yelling, and everyone was excited and upset. Mose's wife Molly had been sitting in front of their house and told Dad to bring me inside. She washed out the cut and put on a bandage and taped it up so I could get home. Somehow, I got a sudden spurt of energy and had no trouble walking after that. For some strange reason, nobody else tried to ride Cricket home that day.

Dad on my bucking horse, Cricket. *(Photo courtesy Phoebe Wynecoop)*

-Chapter 14-
Riding Pigs

Since by now, both horses and cows had nailed me, I was a little leery of them. But we also had several pigs that were worth experimenting with. We often fed the pigs, but we had been told never to go near the old boar. He was big and ugly, and we had no problem with obeying that order. We gave his pen a lot of room.

But one day we found one of the small pigs outside of the pig pen. Wig and Judge jumped on its back and rode it a ways. Well, I thought that looked like fun, so at the next opportune time, I jumped on it myself.

That pig took off like a shot, heading for the corral, while I tried to hold onto what little hair he had. I wasn't doing a very good job of riding him, and was about to fall off, when he suddenly went under the fence. The bottom rail pole peeled me right off his back.

I was willing to bet that if pigs could laugh, he laughed all night. For once, I didn't get cut or hurt, and it had been a real fun ride. But my head was spinning because everything happened so fast. Man, that pig was quick!

I didn't realize, at the time, that I was riding on some pork chops, bacon and ham, but that fast pig sure tasted good several months later.

Chick, the pig-rider. *(Photo Courtesy Phoebe Wynecoop)*

-Chapter 15-
The Electric Fence

We used fences to keep the cattle out of the garden and the hay or oat field. The easiest and most effective fence for that purpose was an electric fence. We put wooden posts into the ground, nailed on an insulator, clamped a wire onto the insulator, hooked it up to a switch box and car battery and, like magic, we had an electric fence.

When the cows walked up to the fence and touched the wire, they'd get a light shock, jerk and step back. Since the fence produced an obvious reaction from the livestock, we had to experiment and find out what it felt like ourselves. Early on we did not have electricity at our house, but that fence sure gave us a good education.

First, we lightly tapped the wire with our hands – and the pulsating sensation was not too bad. Next, we grabbed it, and that gave us a fair jolt. Our final effort, thanks to our cousin Dale, was to stand in the creek bottom with wet feet, then grab the wire. We all joined hands, then the first guy grabbed the fence, and the end person got zapped.

The car battery that drove our electric fence did not have much power, but Uncle Roy's fence did, so we went down there a lot to play. Usually, the last kid to get there ended up on the end of the line and got the biggest shock.

Unfortunately, we didn't have many visitors to show our trick to. But sometimes we got lucky. With the usual taunt, "Come on, it won't hurt," we eventually got some sucker to bite. The newcomer would stand at the end of the line. The result was always as expected – he gave out a loud yelp of surprise at the electric shock. Of course, we knew what to expect, since we all had already taken our turns at the end of the line.

After all of these experiments, we had to try the ultimate test – peeing on the charged electric wire. Since we were not experienced at peeing on something as small as a wire, this required some fine aiming. Once you did hit the wire, you didn't need to see the actual contact to know your aim was on target. Results were quick and "shocking." The first time you tried was the last! That shock was too much to warrant another attempt.

Now that was the ultimate trick to play on some innocent visitor. Out of curiosity, all newcomers and /or non-believers had to try out their aim. The end result was the same – a quick yelp, with the experienced "pee-shockers" laughing heartily at the new victim.

A photo depicting the type of kids who would lure unsuspecting victims to touch an electric fence. In this photo these kids are drinking water from the inlet of a water trough. *(Photo courtesy Phoebe Wynecoop)*

-Chapter 16-
Childhood Diseases

After Wig started school, he brought every kid's disease he could find home to us all. My first round was with German measles, which I caught when I was probably about four years old. I had to stay in bed for a week in a dark room to protect my eyes, so I slept a lot.

One afternoon, while I was sleeping in the folks' room, I woke up and everything was red outside. I started yelling "Fire! Fire! The house is on fire."

The folks ran outside and looked around. Fortunately, there was no fire. I had just been having an extreme reaction to the measles. Dad was especially afraid of fire because he had lost a sister in a house fire.

We kids also caught mumps, chicken pox and the red measles, plus numerous colds and the flu in their respective seasons.

When the mumps hit our family, I was already attending school. Since I was the last kid in our gang waiting to catch the mumps, I had to stay home until I came down with them, giving me a nice long spring break. At that time in 1942 or 1943, if one family member caught a contagious disease, the rest of the family had to stay home until it ran its course. Missing school really bothered me, since I always tried for perfect attendance each year. Perfect school attendance was a goal each of us had, but with all the colds and diseases around, we seldom accomplished it.

Sometime after Dad built the new house, he bought another car. Then we were in business to travel around and see things more than ever before. One of the first trips I remember was going to the hospital in Chewelah. The folks told us that we needed to have our tonsils removed, and I believe four or five of us had them removed at that time.

Once Mom and Dad explained the operation to us, we agreed to go through with it. I think all we heard was, "Ice cream will help your throat feel better after it's over, and you can have all the ice cream you want when we get home."

When the big day of the operations came, a Saturday morning, they loaded us into the car and we headed for the hospital. The trip took an hour. The hospital was a big building, all clean, and it smelled of medicine. Everything seemed okay until I actually got onto the operating table. Then, things got a little scary – especially, when they put that mask over my face and I could smell the ether. Then the nurse asked me to start counting. I didn't make it to thirty before I was out cold.

The next day, we all went home and went to bed. My throat hurt so bad I couldn't even talk. The folks probably really enjoyed the peace and quiet – at least, until we started asking for water and the ice cream we'd been promised. Mom made good on her promise. We were offered vanilla or strawberry flavors and we were served in our beds. Aspergum really helped and in a day or two we were all feeling back to normal.

Judge and Chick, prime candidates for disease. *(Wynecoop photo)*

-Chapter 17-
Starting School

We moved from the log house to our new house in 1941. We had visited the house site many times before, especially during its construction. We followed closely every bit of progress, so we knew all about this place where we were going to live.

Back then, you mixed your own concrete. Dad hauled in the sand and gravel, bought some cement, borrowed a gasoline motor-powered mixer, then mixed the concrete. There was a crew helping Dad, but I am not sure who they were.

We walked on the walkway built on the forms and watched the workmen wheel the concrete around in a wheelbarrow. We started playing in the house even before it was completed.

The new house had electricity, and some indoor plumbing, which was not hooked up to a water source right away. That meant building another outdoor toilet, completely furnished with a Sears Roebuck catalog.

Moving into the new house didn't get us any closer to school. In fact, we were now farther away. Even though the bus went by our gate, we still walked to school. We felt a lot of freedom walking to school, doing things our way.

I knew that little brothers and sisters were allowed to visit on the last day of the school year. So when Judge and his friend Jim "Banjo" headed for school that last day, it had been agreed that I could go with them. I was so excited! I got up early and followed them to school, eager to get a taste of it all.

The big boys didn't seem to mind my going along as long as I didn't get in their way. Once we got there, I couldn't believe I was with so many kids. Kids were everywhere! There must have been at least 70 to 80 kids. Lunch was a big picnic and we had nothing but fun. As far as I was concerned, if that was what school was like, it was going to be more than okay and I couldn't wait to get started.

Since my birthday was on November 3rd, I had to wait until I was almost seven to start school. In the long run, that probably was a positive thing, but at the time I certainly wasn't happy about having to wait so long.

When school started in the fall of 1942, I was more than ready to go. World War II had started the previous year, but we kids didn't really understand what that meant. Our lives as children were not affected much by the war. While many of our older relatives were going into the service, others were doing everything to stay out of it. Some folks in our community were leaving to find work. I guess some things were changing fast around me, but I was mostly just concerned about being old enough to get into school.

School kids Judge and Wig. *(Photo courtesy Phoebe Wynecoop)*

School for me was pure fun – filled with all kinds of new treats – little chairs and tables, coloring books, building blocks and toys. My first real problem was with the little chairs. I kept leaning back and rocking in my chair until one day I went too far and the chair tipped over backwards and we both went under the table.

My teacher, Mrs. Larkin, warned me that the chair might tip over, but of course, I needed to find that out for myself. Back then, teachers held strong control in the classroom. Each one had their set of rules, and you were expected to follow them. If you didn't, you were punished accordingly.

My going under the table was not one of her rule-breakers. The surprise and shock of my downfall provided enough of a lesson learned without further punishment. Man, that was quick! I went under the table and then all the other kids started laughing. Other than being really embarrassed, I wasn't hurt. Mrs. Larkin gave me one of those "I-told-you-so!" looks and only a mild chewing-out.

I got that treatment a couple times for staying out past the end of our recess. Specifically, I didn't get into my own class line to go back into school. Here's why. The older kids' recess started when ours ended. Since I knew a lot of the older kids, I stayed out to play with them. It was fun while it lasted.

Like most kids, the very personal need to go to the bathroom can sometimes be a big concern. Kids were supposed to use the toilet during recess. Any coming and going from the classroom was a major issue for the teacher.

Since the first and second grades were in the same room, one on each side of the room, sometimes it took a while to get your need recognized. My arm would get tired waving, trying to get Mrs. Larkin's attention. I always suspected she ignored me on purpose, thinking I didn't really have to go.

But my persistence usually paid off. The bathroom was pretty nice. It was inside, had toilet paper, flushing toilets and smelled clean. It sure made the old outhouse seem out-of-date.

Another strong memory all of us kids had was about school lunches. The food was generally pretty good, but occasionally they served us the dreaded string beans and/or salmon. The problem was that you had to clean your plate before you could leave the lunch room. That really put a squeeze on us, because we were losing valuable playing time by staying inside to finish the hard-to-take food.

Sometimes, the staff would finally weaken and let us go outside before we had eaten all of the food; other times we'd choke it down to get to go out and play. String beans were the cook's favorite torture.

Since all the little kids had to sit at a little table where the cook could watch us, we didn't get away with much. I will always remember her stern instructions, "You kids eat your string beans." The strings on those beans just were not chewable, and they trailed down my throat until I almost gagged. Several times we had to sit in the lunchroom until class time.

The salmon patties weren't much easier to get down. They were full of little crunchy bones, and when I'd bite into one, it repulsed me. The bones were well-cooked, but the thought of chewing bones bothered me.

Dick and Dave waiting for school. *(Photo courtesy Phoebe Wynecoop)*

I could usually get the salmon down, but it was tough. At mid-afternoon, we often had snacks of dried apples, walnuts and raisins that made up for the awful green beans and salmon.

Being naturally left-handed, I endured other problems in school. Mrs. Larkin tried to make me do everything right-handed. At that time, left-handers were supposed to be converted to right-handedness. It wasn't that easy to convert me. Mrs. Larkin worked pretty hard and gave it her best shot, especially since I was one of only two left-handed students in the room. I'm happy to say she eventually gave up on me.

Writing left-handed caused some other challenges. I either turned the paper, or raised my arm up high on the desk, resulting in an unusual slant to my writing. If the teacher had spent as much time improving my left-handed writing as she did trying to convert me, I could have been great in penmanship.

During penmanship lessons, all my vertical lines would start out vertical, then gradually start tipping over to my unnatural back slant. Of course, that is not what the teacher wanted, so I was corrected. My lines would again be vertical for a while, then they started tipping over again. I never did master vertical lines. I used my fingernail to stop the line on the bottom, but the top looked like uneven grass.

Good students who performed well for the teacher could go into the little back room and play or do some exercises. My penmanship kept me out of the back room more than anything else.

Like all kids, we played a lot of games at school. One of the more popular games was Cowboys and Indians. It's odd, that considering we lived on an Indian reservation and most of us were at least part Indian, no one wanted to be the Indians.

Cowboys were the good guys and Indians were the bad guys. We had learned that from the radio programs that we listened to. At that age, we didn't know we were tribal members, and therefore, the bad guys. Eventually, someone would agree to be an Indian, just so we could get some play in before recess ended.

We liked to play in the trees at school, but we did not swing from tree to tree like we did at our old house. Our cousin Hobie once fell out of a tree while playing at school, so we walked by that tree like it was a holy shrine.

The trees at school were not so good for climbing. After we climbed them, we looked like we'd been wrestling the tree, coming away with bark and dirt all over our clothes.

The teachers would ask what we had been doing, and we would say, "just playing." That was partly true. But we had not been playing on the playgrounds. We were going over the hill below the playground to an area where we were not allowed to go. Of course, we knew that forbidden soil made for the very best playground.

Since the war was raging in Europe and the Pacific, we also acted out a lot of war games, complete with soldiers, nurses and tanks. We'd shoot up the place with our stick guns, and if we were wounded, the nurses came to our aid. In our war games, we were all on the American side. There were only imaginary enemies, so we always won.

Playing marbles was another one of our favorite grade-school games. Every kid had a pocketful or bag of marbles. Some kids even had steelies, usually steel ball bearings. They were heavy and rolled through the circular "pot," scattering marbles everywhere. If the ground was soft, then the steelie was too heavy to go very far. If you knocked an opponent's marble out of the 15- to 18-inch circle, you won the marble. Since steelies were heavy, they were hard to shoot. A small steelie was a prized possession of the marble shooter. Agates were pretty to look at, but no contest for a heavy-duty steelie. There were also large glass "shooter" marbles that could clean out a pot pretty good. But only a steelie could knock another steelie out of the pot.

To shoot marbles well, you had to really develop the right grip. Holding the marble tight in the hook of your first finger, you then pressed it from behind with your thumb. The marble flew out with considerable force, sending your intended prize out of the pot.

To determine the first shooter, we made a mark on the ground and stepped back eight or ten paces, then tossed our marble at the line. Whoever threw closest to the line had the first shot. This was called "lagging."

We also played a marble game called "Chase" that had two players. One guy led off by tossing a marble, then the other guy tried to hit it. If you hit the opponent's marble you won it. If you missed, your opponent could then hit you and win your marble.

Girls seldom played the same games as boys. We all used the playground equipment and played tag together, but girls did not play baseball, softball or football with the boys. And boys didn't play organized sports until the fourth or fifth grade.

When the first year of school was over, we all waited for our report cards, and everyone was happy because next year we would be big second graders. Because my mid-term grades had been good, I wasn't too worried.

When the teacher called out our names, we went up to her desk to get our report card. I opened mine and saw that I had been "promoted." That really confused and upset me, since I didn't know what promoted meant. I was too embarrassed to ask, so after school I started taking the long way home. At my snail's pace, I would never make it by dark. Man, there are a lot of rocks to kick on a country road when you want to kill time!

I met Aunt Ruth coming down the road, and we stopped to talk. Of course, she had to ask if I had passed, and I told her I didn't know because I didn't understand a word on my report card. She asked to see it, so I handed her the card. Then she started laughing. She told me that promoted meant that I had passed and would be in the second grade next year.

What a relief! It felt like a great weight had been taken off my back. I thanked her and ran down through the woods to our house without a worry.

Occasionally, the public health doctor came to the Reservation school and that meant one thing, shots! Oh, how we dreaded getting shots! We had to line up by classroom, so our two-grade classroom made for a long line. The brave ones – usually the girls – went first, and the boys were last.

Part of the problem was that we kids started talking about how the shot was going to hurt, and how the pain would be unbearable, and how a person could die from a shot. After so much of that talk, some of the kids got very pale and sick-looking. Of course, that made it even worse for everyone.

Sometimes a dentist visited the Agency's medical office which truly smelled of medicine and was not a very popular place. For dental checkups and services, we kids had to leave school and walk over to the Agency, which seemed like a lifetime when you didn't know what was waiting for you there. We also had our eyes checked in the same building.

The dentist didn't especially like to fill teeth, but he didn't think twice about pulling out a tooth with a bad cavity. Judging by his speed in going through the line of kids, he must have been paid by head count or the number of teeth he pulled. He pulled two of my molars right after a shot of Novocain.

I can still remember that pain, and for me, a visit to a dentist today is still a white knuckle trip. I sure wish I had brushed my teeth more often when I was young to spare me from many much-feared encounters with dentists later on.

With seven boys, we had an opportunity to refine the tooth pulling process. Pulling our baby teeth at home had been a different kind of challenge for us. When one of us had a loose tooth, we usually worked at it until it came out. But that was not always the remedy. Like other kids, sometimes we tied a string around the tooth, gave a quick jerk, and out it came. Another method of extraction was to tie a string around the tooth, then pull the string tight both ways, really popping that tooth out.

Sometimes, we tied the tooth string to the knob of an open door, then slammed the door shut, yanking the tooth out. Once we even tied a string to our dog, old Tex, and told him to "sic-um" the command to chase a cow. When he ran off after the cow, the tooth came out. With a lot of kids in our family, there were many teeth to pull and just as many ways to do the job.

The person having the tooth pulled didn't always just bravely stand there. Once the decision was made on the pulling technique, it took considerable time to carry out the task. The "victim" whimpered and said that he'd changed his mind. Once the string was on, he would stay real close to the one holding the string. Then someone would have to hold or distract the *pullee* until the *puller* could do his designated job.

But getting back to our good old school days, here's another story about something that has affected me all my life.

One day, the teacher announced that we had a visitor coming who would show us a movie and talk to us about forest fires. That sounded great to me, since anything other than regular classwork was a nice change. When the time rolled around, two men came into the room. They were both tan and had on uniforms. One set up the movie projector, and the other talked about forest fires and how dangerous and destructive they were.

At that time, we had seen very few movies – especially ones in color – so when the movie started, we were all eyes and ears. That movie was great, and the color of the wildlife and outdoor scenery was beyond belief: the strutting prairie chickens, head-butting bighorn sheep, elk, mountain goats and honking geese – all were nothing short of incredible.

Most of the animals were new to us, except for what we'd seen in magazines. But to see them in real living color was something special. Right then and there I decided what I was going to do when I grew up – be a forester.

Winters were long and cold, so since we always walked to and from school, Mom tried making us wear long underwear. It was so scratchy that we complained a lot, so she bought us girl's long stockings and garters to wear underneath. Man, that was it! If you stuck your head out the window, you could still hear us yelling about that injustice.

For a while, we gave in and wore the stockings on bitter, cold days. But compared to the girly stuff, the old, long underwear eventually became more desirable, scratches and all. Obviously, we couldn't take off the stockings or long underwear at school, but it was much too hot to sit still in class all day. We were really dying to get out of the classroom just to cool down a bit.

Clothes were hard to get, so we should have been happy to have anything to wear. The war was starting to have an impact on us, after all. Shoes were especially hard to buy, since the military was using all the leather. Hand-me-downs of wartime shoes were common in most families. They didn't usually fit, so we clomped around the best we could and got some nasty blisters. Maybe that's why we went barefoot so much, weather permitting.

Those war shortages and hand-me-downs also applied to pants, shirts and other clothing. The younger boys each had a turn at wearing the clothes of the older ones. That was okay; we looked forward to wearing the clothes of the bigger kids because that meant we were growing up. Rolled up pants legs were popular then for new and old clothes. That was the style, and we fit right in. We were stylish kids.

Nothing like a cold soda, Dick and Dave. *(Photo courtesy Phoebe Wynecoop)*

-Chapter 18-
Chewing Gum

All of us kids on the Reservation had a relative or family member in the service. Many of my cousins and uncles served in either the army, navy, air force or marines, so we kept track of military action in both the Atlantic and Pacific theaters.

Since Mom and Dad controlled the radio when the news programs came on, we started listening to the news, and we followed the progress of the war like they did. Dad had tried to join the army, but they wouldn't take him. They told him to go home because he had too many kids and a bad eye. He was probably somewhat disappointed about being turned away. But in the long run, I am sure he didn't mind having to stay home.

Uncle Glenn was in the army, stationed in Alaska. Once, when he came home on a furlough, the folks went to Granddad Galbraith's to visit with him. Mom told us that our uncle was going to bring us a surprise. We couldn't imagine what it could be.

There was little to no candy at the Wellpinit store, and sugar was rationed. There were so many necessities and luxuries that we went without in our wartime kids' world. But since Glenn was in the service, he could buy all the treasures we desired at his commissary. The wait to see him and our surprise was, oh, so long. We saw him coming down the hill towards us and we ran up to meet him. He carried a carton of gum – 24 packages of five sticks of gum. What a present! Glenn became our favorite uncle forever.

We treated that gum like it was priceless, and it really was. No one for miles around had any, and it had been so long since we'd chewed a stick, we had forgotten how good it was. That gum caused many a laugh. We would chew one stick all day, stick it on the head of the bed or on the bed post, and chew the same stick the next day. We found out that chewing gum did not lose its flavor on the bedpost overnight. It had already lost its flavor from chewing before it got stuck there.

One morning, I woke up but could not get out of bed. Something was holding me down. Every time I tried to raise my head, the pillow came up. And someone was pulling my hair. What a weird feeling, my head being stuck to the pillow! Sometime during the night, the gum had fallen out of my mouth, landing on my pillow. As I rolled around asleep, my hair, the pillow and gum all got together and I became stuck to the pillow.

What a tragedy – not only getting the pillow case dirty, but losing hair and wasting a stick of perfectly good gum. The first time this happened, I had to call for help. Mom kept telling me to get out of bed or I would be late for school. I kept yelling back, "I can't! I'm stuck in bed." That was worth a few laughs. Mom finally came upstairs to see what was wrong and I was really stuck to the pillow. She had to cut out a gob of my hair to get me loose.

This happened to me more than once. The other times, one of my wiser older brothers got the scissors and cut me loose. My hair looked like the dog had been chewing on it. Dad always gave us our haircuts, so I figured that if I could get to him in time before school, he could at least make my hair look presentable.

Of course, gum and school did not mix. We were not allowed to chew gum in school. If we were caught, the teacher took it away from us. Several times, I wish they would have taken more of it. Here's why! I would put it in my pocket, leave it on our dinner plate, or leave it on the bed post for a day or so, and it would get hard and crumbly and not good to chew anymore. When the teacher took away our gum we made sure we only gave up old chewed gum – not a fresh stick.

I have to admit that during the gumless times of the war years, we tried to chew the black pitch from pine trees. That's how desperate we were. The flavor of that stuff was terrible, but if you could chew and spit enough, the pitch taste eventually went away. It might take 10 to 15 minutes of chewing on the worst tasting stuff there ever was to get the desired effect, but we did it.

After you chewed pine pitch for a while, when you took it out of your mouth, it started to crumble. That was the end of it and you had to throw it away. Then your only choice was to start on another chunk – after you'd pulled out the pine needles, bark and moss, of course. Was it worth it? I guess so. We did what we had to do.

Handsome Chick, with slick hair, before the chewing gum attack.
(Photo courtesy Phoebe Wynecoop)

-Chapter 19-
Picking Berries

As I said earlier, many things were scarce for us during the war. But with a large family, we qualified for a lot of rationing stamps. Dad was now in the logging business and that helped, too. Tires and gasoline were hard to come by, but the logging and ranching provided extra stamps for gas that we could use for necessary trips.

During our free time, we picked a lot of wild berries for jams and jellies. Wild strawberries grow on plants right on the ground and are so small that most people don't see them. But, they have such a wonderful flavor that they are worth the effort of searching for them. Getting a cupful in a day meant you'd had good picking.

When Mom told us that we had enough sugar to make jam, we took a glass or cup and headed to where we knew we could usually find strawberries. A-berry-picking we would go. We really appreciated eating wild strawberry jam on fresh, hot homemade rolls, but it seemed to take forever to pick enough to make a batch of jam. When I was old enough to drive the jeep (13-14 years old), Mom and all of us kids wandered the hills in the early summer, trying to come up with a cup of wild strawberries between us.

There's nothing like the smell of fresh baked bread in a house, especially when you know there is fresh jam or jelly to put on it. Mom was/is a great bread baker, and we all appreciated her baking talent.

Huckleberries grow in various sizes, large and small, but are easier to pick than wild strawberries. They grow on bushes one to three feet tall in large patches. Everyone liked to pick huckleberries. Blue fingers are the marks of a good huckleberry picker, and blue lips and teeth always show a good huckleberry eater.

We had to travel some distance to pick huckleberries, and the trip made it more fun. Once you eat them, you never forget their strong, very distinctive flavor. To me, they make the best jam.

We also had fun picking raspberries when we had a chance. Those raspberries were big, too, and the bushes grew tall. Once, I went to Spokane with Aunt Amy and Uncle Merritt and helped them pick raspberries.

Another time, we all crawled into the hay-filled back of the old Reo truck and headed for the mountains to pick huckleberries. That night, we ate fried chicken, rolls and beans while sitting around a small campfire. Since we didn't have a tent, we slept rolled up in blankets in the hay in the truck bed.

When lying on your back looking up on a dark, clear night you can see so many stars that the heavens seem to go on forever. Although we didn't find many berries on that trip, we sure had a lot of fun. That outing confirmed my decision on my future career, being a forester. I imagined what a life that would be – camping out and living in the mountains.

We had to use some of our rationing stamps to get sugar, which was in scarce supply. Walking up to the store with the coupons to buy what Mom wanted was a real responsibility. If you lost the stamps, you were in for it, because they could not be replaced.

There were different kinds of rationing stamps for different items, and with eight people (six kids and the parents) we got a lot of stamps. I can remember going to the store and taking out several of the coupon books and handing them to Uncle Roy or Aunt Christine, the storekeepers, so they could tear out the stamps he needed. We kept careful track of each and every stamp, because they were worth more than money. They got us supplies that money couldn't buy.

One morning before school, I went to the store for Mom to get some fly repellant. I was in a hurry, because I didn't want to be late to class. Coming down the trail towards our place, I noticed that my arm felt wet. I could smell that some fly spray had leaked out onto my skin. As I got closer to the house, my arm started to burn and turn red.

By the time I made it home, I was in major pain. We tried to wash it off, but that didn't work. It was too late – the damage had been done. Mom put some lotion on it and that helped, but it burned like fire all day. I still went to school, but I was in agony all day. I kept washing it, and eventually after several days, the burning went away. That was some powerful spray. For a while, flies fell to the ground when I passed by.

We all did our best to help the war efforts. We picked up all the old metal we could find and turned it in. I'm not sure who collected the metal, but we piled it up and Dad took it somewhere. We collected tin cans, glass, aluminum, twine, tin foil, etc. There was always a scrap metal drive going on at the Agency.

In our efforts to clean up the countryside, we discovered a lot of old rusted cars with chrome hood ornaments, so we soon started collecting the ornaments. We had so many different kinds, from little chrome figures to fancy designs that had been imbedded in glass and fastened to the hood. They were hard to remove, and we broke some of them in the removal process.

These hood ornaments were really nice, but we couldn't find enough of them to make up a decent collection, so that project went by the wayside. Car bodies were all taken to be melted down for the war effort, and our hood ornaments disappeared into the metal pile with the other scrap metal. Sometimes, I wonder how much that small collection would be worth today.

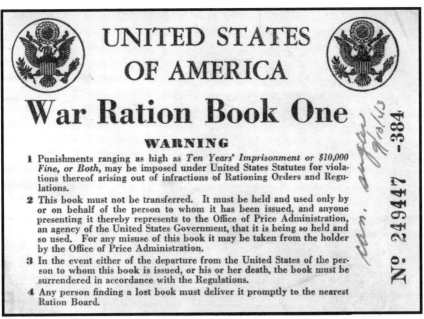

War ration book.

-Chapter 20-
Preparing for War

When the war started in the Pacific, that meant that it was even closer to us. Since we were near the West Coast, we figured we would have to join in and fight. So we dug foxholes on the hill across from the house. We worked hard on those foxholes – dug them two to three feet deep and several feet across. We were more than ready for an enemy attack!

Wig and Tex. Tex is waiting for his next victim. *(Photo courtesy Phoebe Wynecoop)*

We spent quite a bit of time and energy developing our defensive positions for the imminent attack that never came. Once when we were manning the foxholes, we heard our dog Tex barking and saw him jumping around over in the trees. We ran over to see what he had.

It was a big rattlesnake coiled up on the ground. With sticks and rocks we finished off that old snake, but the idea that there had been a rattlesnake that close to our play area and home made us more careful. Tex killed another rattlesnake once while we were hunting birds. (Don't worry, even more rattlesnake stories will come later.)

Meanwhile, back to the foxholes. We kept our eyes glued to the western sky and watched for signs. A red sky meant there was a bloody battle somewhere out there, and with several cousins out in the Pacific, we worried about them and all the Americans in the war.

-Chapter 21-
Christmas Celebrations

Christmas was a great time for us, but we knew that because of the war, our haul of presents would not be very big – not that we were expecting much, anyway. We really looked forward to Christmas activities at school and church.

At school, we drew names in our class and brought a little present for the person whose name we drew. That was always exciting, because you didn't know who had your name.

The big event at school was the Christmas play – especially in grade school. The stage was at one end of the gymnasium, and chairs were lined up on the gym floor where all of our families and the whole community sat to watch the performance.

Every grade put on a skit and all students had a line or two to say. Each class stayed in its room until the big moment. Then we filed down the backsteps of the school and onto the stage for our part of the performance.

Wellpinit Presbyterian Church. *(Photo courtesy Phoebe Wynecoop)*

While the curtain was closed, we were okay. Then, when the curtain opened, stage fright was our main action – or reaction. Everyone stood frozen in shock. We could hardly remember our names, let alone our lines. Like most kids, we spent more time looking for our families than remembering our lines. But after a while we all calmed down and did our things and went back to our room.

Back in the classroom, each of us got a brown paper bag filled with mixed nuts, candy and an apple or an orange. Now that was something special! Like I said, with the war on, any kind of fruit was a real treat.

Church Christmas programs were comparable but different. The local Presbyterian Church which we belonged to seemed so big. All the town turned out at Christmas. People especially gathered by the big old stove in the back corner of the church, since that was the warmest spot in the building.

There was always a big Christmas tree up in the front of the church. It was lightly decorated with homemade ornaments and chains made of strips of colored paper. No one had electric Christmas tree lights, so paper stars hung all over the tree to brighten it up.

All of us Sunday School kids had our own verses to recite, and when our turn came we had to walk up to the altar in front of God and everyone and say our piece. It seemed like those one-line verses were the hardest thing to memorize, especially when you started learning them only an hour before your turn in front of the whole church.

Lighting was poor and the stage area was very small and cold, but we knew there would be one present for each of us, so we held on and somehow made it through the program.

As the evening wore on, the excitement level rose. From the number of presents under the tree, we each hoped we might be lucky and get more than one. After waiting for what seemed like an eternity, each name was finally called and we received a small present. Wig was in the Air Force and his present was khaki shorts, size 44. He was size 32.

Mr. Lee and Mr. Wasson are the two ministers I remember. Albert Sam was a local man who led most of the services, especially on Christmas Eve. He was tall and stood up in front of the congregation and lead the singing or gave a sermon.

Albert Sam. *(Photo Courtesy "Children of the Sun")*

Albert would occasionally talk about his meeting the Lord. He'd been sitting in the Spokane city jail, listening to the people singing in the church across the street. That had inspired and encouraged him to give up drinking and carousing and to become a Christian. That he did, and Albert Sam was a great inspiration to the Reservation Presbyterian community. I can still hear him singing the hymn "My Hope is Built on Nothing Less," with the chorus ending, "On Christ, the solid rock I stand, all other ground is sinking sand."

Our church was considered a mission church. Our sponsoring church in Spokane, First Presbyterian, gave each of us kids a Christmas gift, usually clothing, which we certainly appreciated. It wasn't so much the present that meant a lot to us, but it was the idea that someone would send it to a total stranger. That's what made it special.

We also received a brown paper bag of candy, nuts and an apple or orange like we did at school. We knew that, considering how scarce everything was, someone in Spokane had given up a lot so we could have that Christmas treat. With an orange from the school and an apple from the church, we felt like we had it made.

The school program was usually several days before Christmas, and the church program was always on Christmas Eve. Once the church festivities were completed, we were about worn out. We usually got home pretty late on the night before Christmas.

Dad never went to the school or church programs, but he usually came to pick us up afterwards. The car was warm and we were tired but excited, and we were more than ready to go to bed.

When we were young, Mom and Dad took us out into the woods to cut down our Christmas tree. We always started with a big argument at each tree we came upon because we couldn't agree on the perfect tree. After walking through the snow for an hour or so, it became easier to agree on a tree. We finally ended up picking out a tree that probably wasn't as good as some that we couldn't agree on earlier.

Once we got the tree into the house, it usually looked so thin you could have thrown a cat through it and never touched a limb. But we made do with our final choice, no matter what.

We all had to help decorate the tree. The popular icicles were easy to put on, but with so many small kids at work, most of the silver stuff ended up on the bottom. Tree candles were popular at that time, but Mom and Dad would not allow candles on our tree. Too many houses had burned down from these dangerous decorations. And, as I said before, Dad had lost a sister in a house fire, so he was always extra careful with fire.

Once the tree was up and decorated with icicles, paper chains from school, some small colored glass balls, and a star on top, all we had to do was wait until Christmas morning. In later years we had bubble lights. They were pretty, but it was hard to make them stand up.

As we got older, the folks had enough of our "looking for the perfect tree" argument and sent us kids out by ourselves to find a tree. We kids had better luck finding a tree on our own, since only a couple of us went and there were fewer opinions to sort out.

Waiting for Christmas morning to come was the hard part. We thought we knew what presents we wanted to get and had worn out the Christmas catalogs looking for them. But we changed our minds every day, and by the time Christmas rolled around, it didn't matter one bit what we got.

Back on the home front, around Christmas we seemed to migrate towards one bed. I'm not sure why. Probably, that made it easier to tell stories or to discuss our Christmas list, when we were all clumped together like that.

Once in bed, we tried our best to go to sleep, but then someone made a noise. Somebody else said, "Did you hear that?" Then everyone was wide awake again, sure that we had heard Santa's sleigh on the roof. We would run to the window and look for Santa, but no one was ever there. This happened several times until we finally fell asleep. I know that I heard the sleigh runners one night. I was so sure of it that today I can close my eyes and still hear those runners on our roof.

We were told not to come downstairs on Christmas morning until it was daylight. But we crowded that limit. Once, I was up at 2:30 a.m..- it looked light enough outside to me. After I'd boldly led the charge downstairs, Mom and Dad made us all go back up to bed until dawn's early light.

Then, when Christmas finally dawned, we couldn't open any presents until the cows were fed, the cow was milked, the wood was cut and the water was carried. Those holiday mornings we were really fast with our chores. As we got older, we often ate breakfast before opening presents.

After opening our gifts, we usually played with or admired our new possessions, and then we worked on jigsaw puzzles or played checkers, Chinese checkers, Monopoly, or went skating. Our day was always topped off with a big meal at Granddad's or one Mom cooked at home.

Christmas dinner was usually mid-afternoon and we enjoyed turkey, dressing, mashed potatoes, sweet potatoes, homemade rolls, strawberry jam, pumpkin pie and a fruit salad. What a feast!

Granddad's Christmas tree was always really thin – on purpose. While we kids tried to find the bushiest tree, Granddad always looked for one with the fewest limbs. Although his tree was thin, it was decorated just right, really pretty.

We each usually received a book from Grandma – some boy's story about airplanes, cowboys and adventures. There were other traditional gifts given in our family. In later years, we gave each other gifts like gloves, hats, earmuffs, and such.

-Chapter 22-
School Activities

Valentine's Day was also a fun day at school, because it was when your popularity was determined. The kid with the most valentines was obviously the most popular. The cards from the girls were the most important to us boys. We were usually embarrassed by the cards, but they were fun to get.

We boys were very careful about the wording on any card or a piece of candy we gave a girl. Why? Because she might just misunderstand the message, and you could end up with a girlfriend. That would be real bad.

One spring day after school, we were loaded into a car and taken down to the old fairgrounds to attend our first Boy Scout meeting. There we would learn all about the great outdoors, how to survive in the woods, make crafts and read a compass. That really sounded great to us, especially since we would also get to wear a uniform at a later date.

After the meeting, the scout leader walked us around through the woods, like we had never been there. After some time wandering around, he was lost. We knew where we were, but he didn't believe us, so all of us prospective scouts headed out. We went over to the old railroad track and ran up to the school. That ended the Boy Scouts organization efforts on our Reservation. It was too bad that the program was dropped, because we lost our big chance to wear uniforms.

When the school yard was covered with snow, we played "Fox and Geese" and threw snowballs outside. But in really bad weather, we were usually allowed to play in the gym. Of course, we couldn't wear our normal shoes in there – they had to be white rubber-soled shoes. Black soles were banned because they left black marks everywhere. The other option was to take off your shoes. The floor was then so slick that you spent most of your time on the floor. We still had fun playing tag, running and sliding, and the rough and tumble game, "Red Rover, Red Rover... Send Johnny Over."

There was always a basketball laying around the gym, but it was so big and hard that it could knock you down or hurt your hands. I'd watched the big kids play and admired how they threw the ball through the basket that seemed way too high. I tried to throw the ball at the basket, but it was too heavy. Some of the kids used an underhand shot, so I started doing that. I still couldn't reach the basket, but I came a lot closer. As I grew, it became easier to reach the basket and in later years, basketball was one of my favorite games to play and watch.

One morning when I was in the fourth of fifth grade, someone knocked on the classroom door. The teacher answered it, and after some discussion, she told me to get my coat and boots and to go to the school office. I was pretty nervous and a little scared by the time that I got to the office. But since Uncle Jack Knoll was the superintendent, I wasn't too worried. Wig was there with my cousin Lorena. Uncle Jack said we were to go on a field trip for the day – to tour Grand Coulee Dam.

We were really surprised, but eagerly agreed to go. Five of us crawled into the station wagon bus with Uncle Jack and away we went.

We got almost to Reardan when the road got real bad and filled with deep, muddy ruts. After we kids got out and figured out the best route, Uncle Jack maneuvered the bus through the mud. Then we climbed back on board.

Once we got to Reardan, we stopped to get gas. The station attendant said, "How did you guys get here?" Uncle Jack said, "We just drove down from Wellpinit." The guy was really surprised and said, "You're the first ones through that didn't get stuck." Then he said, "But you're from Wellpinit. You guys are born in the mud and know how to drive in it." I wasn't sure if he had insulted us or was paying us a compliment.

We went on to tour Grand Coulee Dam, learned a lot there about electricity and electrical power, and made it home after school was out. This excursion made me feel a little different, because someone had thought enough of me to give me some special treatment. Thanks, Uncle Jack.

The school was the main entertainment center of the community. Aside from high school sports and the children's Christmas plays, the adults held dances, and played cards there. Pinochle was the adults' favorite card game. Everyone liked to dance and play cards. When relatives came from out of town, I got to baby-sit. I'd go up to Granddad's and watch one or two kids while the adults were over at the school for some special event. Since my grandparents' house was close to the school, we had a signal. I would turn on the back porch light if something went wrong with the baby-sitting.

Once, my cousin Johnny Sutton stuck his head through the bars at the foot of the bed and I couldn't get him out. The mattress was too high and I couldn't push it down enough so that he could get his head out. I didn't really want to turn on the porch light, but after many tries, I finally gave up on freeing him and I turned on the porch light. Johnny's mom, my Aunt Gertrude, came to his rescue pronto.

I liked baby-sitting, because I was allowed to stay at Granddad's place overnight, sleep in a big bed, and read some of their old magazines. Of course, it also meant that the adults knew that I was growing up and was ready for bigger responsibilities.

Amateur hour programs were also held at the school. Local people would sing and/or play a musical instrument or perform some other act. After the war, they added bubble gum blowing contests to the programs. The kid who could blow the biggest bubble won a prize.

At that time, bubble gum was just becoming available and popular again. I must admit that I had perfected bubble blowing to an art. I mixed bubble gum and regular gum and what a bubble that made! I practiced and practiced. Huge bubbles blew up in my face and stuck to my hair, eyebrows, cheeks and nose, but it was fun. Picture that!

When the big night of the contest came, I was ready. I could hardly wait for the announcer to say, "The next event is the bubble blowing contest." All of us contestants were so excited that when the time came to go up on the stage, our mouths were so dry we couldn't have blown a bubble if our lives depended on it.

After some really heavy chewing, little bubbles started coming out. Once I relaxed, I did get one of my record-size bubbles out. I won first prize. Wow! I was the local bubble-blowing champ! All the old gum-in-the-hair days paid off, after all.

When we became 6th graders, we qualified for a real bonus at the school. After basketball practice or a game, we could take a shower in the school gym's dressing room. Man, that was great – no more wash tub. I could stand in that shower forever because I didn't have to carry water to it. All the boys enjoyed taking showers at the gym.

We all learned how to snap each other with a wet towel. Of course, that really hurt, but pain was part of the game. Some of the towels really

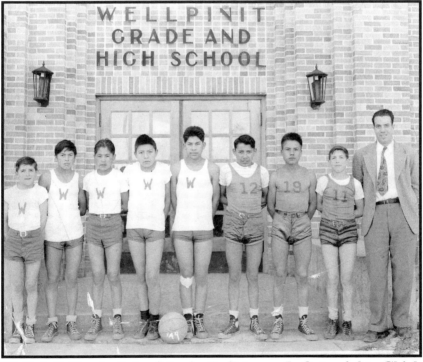

Wellpinit Grade School basketball team. Left to right: Chick Wynecoop, Mel Peone, Albert Brown, Carson Sherwood, Thomas Sam, Jim Wynne, Andrew Bohn, Judge Wynecoop, and Coach Glenn Galbraith. *(Wynecoop photo)*

smelled sour. Everyone brought a towel from home, but I believe some never changed towels all year. As the year wore on, the smell of dirty towels was stronger than the wet bodies they dried off and much worse than anybody's body odor. Using the dirty towel made you smell worse than not taking a shower.

Up until the time we were old enough to take a shower at school, we had to take a bath at home in a wash tub. To do that took a considerable amount of water that had to be heated on the wood stove. Some of the wood kitchen stoves had a water tank alongside the stove's fire chamber that did a pretty good job of heating up the water.

Of course, bath night meant extra water had to be carried. Taking a bath at home meant taking off your clothes, which was embarrassing. For some reason, taking showers at school was different. Since most of the boys were all naked at the same time, we quickly became used to seeing naked guys and didn't gawk too much.

"Bath day." Steve, Dick, Wig and Dave with dirty little Chick or Judge in the tub. *(Phoebe courtesy Wynecoop)*

-Chapter 23-
Water Problems

Getting enough water to meet all of our needs was still a problem. Our new house didn't have running water, so we had to carry water from a spring over by a small creek. Someone had dug a hole and put a short piece of culvert standing up into the ground. I'd put the bucket into the water, and by tipping it over, it would sink and fill up.

The culvert was small and I had to wait for the pipe to fill up before I could fill another bucket. While waiting for the pipe to fill, I headed down the trail for the house with the first bucket. When I got tired, I put the bucket down and went back for the other one. Once I filled that bucket I would carry it to the other one, and after a short rest, I carried both buckets down through the trees and around the bushes to the house. That was my system for water gathering.

The total trip was over 100 yards, so it was quite a job. I had to have all the buckets filled before I left for school. I am sure that I occasionally had help with that chore, especially on wash day.

Another family sometimes used the spring, and that was okay. Occasionally, I'd see the older lady, Mrs. Haines, who lived near the culvert with two boys my age. I know one was her grandson, but I'm not sure about the other one.

Once I was in the tree house up the draw above the well singing in what I thought to be Indian (some concoction I had made up of various sounds). When I looked down, there was Mrs. Haines. She seldom spoke English. She mostly spoke Spokane Salish language, so I really felt dumb. She probably laughed all the way home. At least I must have added some humor to her day.

Sometimes Judge was supposed to help me carry water, and since he was bigger, he was good help. But, often as not, as we started down the trail, we'd get into an argument, and he'd take off running. That made me furious.

There was an old junk pile above the trail. On one occasion, I picked up an old high heeled shoe from it and threw it at him. I was so mad that I missed him by 20 feet. It hit a tree instead, and the shoe bounced off the tree, and hit him on the head. He immediately started bleeding profusely. Listening to him yell and scream, you would think he had been mortally injured.

It was only a small poke from a shoe nail, so the bleeding soon stopped, but it really scared us. I was getting the reputation for throwing things to defend myself, mostly for survival.

Once Dad and Uncle Roy tried to find water near the house by witching. Dad used a willow stick and Roy used a copper wire, and between them they decided where to dig a well. The project was started with great expectations by all – especially the water carriers. We each had our turn digging the new well, which was about four feet across. Finally, we got so deep we needed a windlass to haul out the dirt.

A windlass is a lifting machine, its frame holds a round wood drum 12-15 inches across with a rope wrapped around it. A bucket is hooked to one end of the rope and the other is tied to the center of the drum. There is a handle on one end, and by cranking it, a person could raise or lower the bucket.

The digger put one foot into the bucket and grabbed the rope and stepped off the edge of the hole. Whoever had the windlass handle had to be ready because the bucket went down real fast. By holding the handle tight, you could control the descent of the bucket. With someone down in the hole, you had to be careful and not drop the bucket on the person below. Usually, the bigger and stronger guys stayed on top and the smaller guy went down below.

Even after many days of digging with a pick and shovel, we never hit the amount of water the witching indicated. We stopped digging at 40 feet, with only a trickle of water coming in. Dad put a four-foot culvert inside the well so it wouldn't cave in.

After all our work, the amount of water was hardly worth the effort. Once the pipes were all installed and the pump was hooked up, we had some water, but only enough for the kitchen. We knew that if we ran the well dry, the pump would lose its prime and not pump any water. When that happened, we had to wait for the foot valve to be covered with water and then take a cap off the pipe, pour it full of water, quickly put the cap back on and tighten it, so it would draw the water up. That was a real pain and nuisance. Unfortunately, we went through this necessary ordeal often.

The water witching had not worked very well. We had dug a well in decomposed granite – the last place you would look for water. I am sure that almost anywhere else would have been a better place to dig. The little water we found was good, but it came in too slow.

After our neighbor, Mose Phillips', house burned down, Dad bought his land and improved and expanded Mose's water system. There was a water line from another spring, near our spring, where we fetched water to our house. Dad re-built Mose's old system, putting in a new line to replace the old one. He also put a faucet over by the barn, which came in handy for drinking and watering the stock. He then ran a line to our well, which ran steady to keep the well supplied with water.

That solved most of the water problems, as we could then take a bath more often and even connect the inside toilet. By then, we were taking showers at school and also swimming in the lakes and creeks. The new water system made running the house a whole lot easier.

-Chapter 24-
Summer Chores

Summer was a very busy time. We did a lot of playing, but we also had our chores to do. In the summer, haying was the biggest job. Dad helped a lot, but haying was usually left up to us boys. The oldest was the boss; that's just the way it was. We cut hay, and raked it into long rows called windrows. Then Dad or Wig used the old truck-tractor with a bull rake on the front, and hauled the hay to the barn. A bull rake was made of long wooden poles spaced like a flat basket. It function was to gather a wagon load of hay and move it to the barn.

Cutting hay was the dangerous part of the job. In early years, the mower was pulled by a tractor and someone rode on the mower. The mower rider's job was to step on a lever to raise the sickle bar up and over dirt piles, rocks, and anything else that might be in the way. This was important, because if you hit or cut something other than the hay, the sickle would eventually get dull or its teeth would fall out.

There was a seat on the mower, but when we first started helping with this chore, our legs were too short and we did not weigh enough to push down the lever enough to raise the bar to clear high objects. We were only a notch above no rider. We would grudgingly ride the mower, but it was rough, and I didn't do a very good job of mower bar-raising.

Once, when Dad was pulling the mower and I was riding to raise the sickle bar, I was getting a little bored, so I started watching the grass fall as it was cut. Occasionally, a big sweet clover would go by and I'd reach across the mower wheel and try to catch the clover. That happened one time too many. One time, when an especially tall clover came at me, I reached out to catch it, but I lost my balance and started to fall in front of the mower. It's a good thing that Dad was watching me and stopped the tractor just in time.

When the tractor stopped, the sickle stopped because the power for the sickle comes from the mower's wheels. I regained my balance and we went on. Dad later showed me his scarred legs. As a youth cutting hay with a team of horses, he had once stopped the team to clean the sickle. Then the team had moved, knocking him down. The metal-toothed sickle moved back and forth, cutting up his legs pretty bad. That same thing – or worse – could have happened to me.

The mowing machine was potentially dangerous to animals, too. We usually tried to keep our dogs and cats up at the house when we were mowing. But this didn't always work. Tim, our small black cocker spaniel, was down in the field one day when Dad was cutting hay. Dad didn't see Tim and cut his hind legs so badly that he had to put him out of his misery.

Dad didn't tell us about the accident right away. When we heard the sad news, we were really upset. Later that day we buried Tim across from the house. He was a nice dog and fun to play with. It was a real sad day when we lost Tim to the mower.

Tim had lived to hunt. He hunted birds anytime, anywhere. He also was great for starting fights. When he was with old Tex and they met another dog, Tim jumped on the other dog and started a fight for Tex to finish. Poor Tex got all the scars for fighting Tim's fights.

But let's get back to my tractor tales. Riding the rake was rough, but that was my favorite job. You sat up high, and as the rake filled with hay, you kicked a small lever and it allowed the rake teeth to come up, leaving the hay behind in a pile or windrow. You had to time it so that the hay was always left next to the previous pile. In this way, the hay formed long patterns across the field.

I usually stood in front of the seat, where I was able to kick the release. As I said, the tractor ride was rough. Sometimes the rake would kick up and hit the back of the metal seat, so you had to keep your hands away from there. The teeth on the rake would kick up so hard that I always feared that if they hit my hand or finger, they would have easily cut or broken them.

If the tractor driver pulling the rake picked up speed and went fast, the rake really kicked up and you had to hang on and watch out for those teeth. If you went too fast, the rake skipped a lot of hay, so we generally moved at a fairly slow speed.

After the hay was lined up in neat rows, the next step was for someone to drive a wagon or bull rake down the row, gathering the hay. Then it was taken to the barn or to a haystack.

At the end of the open sided hay barn below the new house was a place clear of grass where we spread three chains out on the ground. The ends were hooked together by a ring that was put over a metal pin in the ground. The other end of the chain or net was hooked to a cable or large rope, then up the end of the barn to a carriage suspended on a track high in the barn. The carriage track ran the length of the barn to the end stop. A cable was hooked through the carriage and out the far end of the barn and hooked to a tractor.

A load of hay was pushed onto the chains, and the end hooked to the metal pin in the ground was disconnected, pulled over the hay, and hooked onto the other end, where there was another hook with a lever attached. Next, a small rope was attached to the lever or trip mechanism. Then, as the large rope was pulled by a tractor at the far end of the barn, the hay was lifted off of the ground and up to the carriage.

When the net hit the carriage, a lock released and the carriage rolled through the barn. When it reached the drop point, the person back at the point of loading pulled the small rope and the trigger released, letting the net fall loose on one end, so the hay fell into the barn. The hay was then leveled and sloped to the outside wall for protection against rain.

This usually worked, but sometimes the hook wouldn't release. Then you went bouncing along because the tractor driver couldn't see you. An alert tractor driver noticed if something wasn't working and stopped until the carriage was tripped. Once tripped, the rope was used to pull the carriage back and down so that the whole operation could be repeated.

At that time, Dad was also running a small logging company and he'd bring in a big tractor to pull up the hay. If the tractor driver didn't watch out, he could have easily pulled the barn over. The worst possible problem was when the chain came loose or released early and pulled out from under the hay. If that happened, you had to move all the hay off and re-hook the chains.

The tractor driver had it made. His job was the best of all. He'd drive forward until the hay was dumped and then back up while the person in the back of the barn was pulling the carriage and rope or cable back by hand. During the back and forth movement of the tractor, sometimes Judge or Dick would step off onto the cat tracks and walk as the tracks moved forward or backward. That was great fun until the folks found out, and we had a discussion on the proper use of dangerous equipment.

We kids were told to stack the edges and smooth out the center of the piled hay. As the barn filled up, the rafters that connected across the barn created a small tunnel. There was also a board down the middle of the barn like the hay shed at the log house. This board did not run the length of the barn. Once the barn was full, in our free time, we'd crawl inside the barn and widen the tunnels. The more we played, the larger the tunnels became.

There were boards nailed to the sides of the barn up about ten to twelve feet, higher than a horse could reach. Our tunnels came to the outside of the barn above those boards, all except for one which you could reach from lower down.

The entrances to the tunnels were not obvious, especially the one at the end of the board in the top of the barn. That entrance went straight down ten to twelve feet, so we entered the tunnel system on top, but couldn't get out that way.

A typical hay storage operation of the times. This was the fastest and most common way to get large amounts of hay into the barns. *(Photo courtesy James Bolser)*

-Chapter 25-
Mose is Stranded

Hay in the barn was always dry, but the tops of the haystacks outside got wet from the fall rains and were covered with snow during the winter. When the wet tops of the haystack froze solid, we'd take a hay saw and cut off a strip of the top to get at the dry hay underneath. A hay saw was an important possession, and we often loaned our saw to others.

Old Mose was a great neighbor. He always walked everywhere, whistling some Indian song, but we could never figure what he was whistling. He came over to the barn often to look around or to borrow tools whenever he wanted. He knew where everything was, especially the hay saw and tongs.

One day while we were at school, Mose came over to borrow the hay saw. He thought it was up in the barn, so up the side of the barn he went. He started walking down the center board, and when he reached the end, he stepped off into the hay and down he went! Into the end of the main tunnel. He crawled to the end of each tunnel, trying to get out and even tried to go up through the hole that he'd fallen into.

But Mose was trapped. It was quite a drop to the bottom of the tunnel, and he just could not get out. He went to the edge, and it was too high to drop to the ground. It was also too high to drop down from where we'd been taking hay out.

He spent the whole afternoon in the barn. Unfortunately, he didn't know about the hidden tunnel entrance. Mom finally heard a feeble voice down at the barn and went down and helped him escape from our death trap.

Mose walked with Mom up to the house and went in and sat down at the dining room table. He was bitching and moaning about being stuck in the barn and how hard it was for an old man to get out. Mom never said, "Maybe you shouldn't have been there in the first place," but she sure thought about it.

Tex had been lying peacefully in the corner, but as Mose became more

Mose Phillips *(Photo courtesy "Children of the Sun")*

livid, Tex got up and walked over to him. That dog started smelling around Mose's chair, then he started to check out Mose's leg. After smelling his leg and shoes, Tex hiked his leg and peed on Mose's shoe.

Mose jumped up and kicked at Tex, who was making a quick exit around the corner. Mose was furious, but the damage had been done. Mose groused around for a bit longer, then left, still a friend. But he never went near the barn again without first checking with someone about borrowing the hay saw. Dad chewed on us pretty hard about our tunnels, but later we had a good laugh about the "Hay Saw Incident."

The new barn was taller, longer and held a lot more hay than the log house barn. The open end of the barn was a great place to play games like "hide and seek," and "king of the mountain." It was also the perfect place for wrestling or just jumping around.

One fall day, a bunch of us were out heading for hay play. I was the first one up to the open end of the barn. As I ran and jumped onto a board on the side of the barn, there was a loud buzzing sound. The next person behind me heard the noise, too. If you've ever heard a rattlesnake, you'll immediately recognize that sound.

I had jumped right over and landed above the rattler, and it was coiled up for the next performance. But either Wig, Judge or Peter Dinehart got a stick and pulled the snake out. For some reason, someone had a .22 rifle handy and they shot that big black diamondback. We were pretty shaken, but after getting so charged up, we looked all over the place for other rattlers that day, but never found one.

We had been around some rattlesnakes before, but they were not very common around the home place. We were always on the lookout for more because we knew how dangerous they were.

-Chapter 26-
More New Chores

Once school started, everything settled down to a routine and we were given new chores to do. Since the water problem had been partially solved, I now became the wood cutter. All I had to do was keep the kitchen stove and the furnace supplied with wood. But that old furnace could burn a lot of wood, and so could the kitchen stove, just like back at the old house.

Our open, unfinished basement was where we stored firewood. That's where I cut the wood for particular uses. Lighting was poor down there, so swinging that big old double bit ax, I had many a near miss. I cut the kitchen stove wood one-handed. On the back swing, I'd occasionally hit one of the rafters, and then I never knew where the ax might go. That's how I gained a few small scars.

When I was in the eighth grade, I was cutting that way when the end of the handle hit the top of the stick I was cutting and I cut a good-sized chunk of skin off my right thumb.

That was bad timing. Baseball season was just starting and now I wouldn't be able to wear a baseball glove. For that injury, my folks took me to the doctor in Reardan. He put a circular pad on the side of my thumb, taped it up tight, and told me to come back in ten days. At the end of a week, my hand smelled so bad I couldn't stand it. I'd sit at my desk at the back of the schoolroom, with my right hand hanging down near floor level to avoid the strong odor.

When the ten days was finally up, Uncle Merritt and Aunt Amy had to go to town, so they gave me a ride back to see the doctor. My uncle didn't like blood, so he wouldn't go into the operating room with me, but my aunt did.

At first, I didn't understand why I had to take my pants off. They gave me a shot of Novocain in my right leg and in my injured hand. Then the doctor told us he would take a piece of skin off of my thigh and graft it onto my thumb.

Wig using a Swedish fiddle (crosscut saw), with Steve riding on the log being sawed. *(Photo courtesy Phoebe Wynecoop)*

I was put on the operating table and partially covered with a cloth, with only my thumb and thigh exposed. The removal of the skin from my leg went okay, but the repair to my thumb wasn't so smooth. The doctor kidded me by saying, "If you could do that good with an ax, what could you do with a scalpel?" Ha, ha. I wasn't laughing. When he stitched the skin to my thumb, it really hurt – especially when the medication started to wear off.

The skin graft eventually healed, and the only permanent damage I suffered was not being able to play baseball that year. At least, I learned how to keep score in a baseball scorebook. And, I got sidelined from doing a lot of chores.

Once I was down in the basement gathering wood, I tripped on a stick and fell down and hit something that ended up being a crosscut saw leaning up against the wall. My right wrist started stinging. I raised it up to have a better look in the dim light and saw two gashes several inches long looking back at me. Those stripes ran pretty deep, but they weren't bleeding yet. I didn't want to look at those jagged cuts, but I had to.

I ran upstairs and Mom put a bandage on them. The saw was really sharp and had done its job well. Unfortunately, it had cut up my arm, not the intended piece of wood.

As I mentioned earlier, Nurse Mom usually took care of our cuts and injuries. Several times I expected Mom to pass out or at least sit down, but our brave mom never did. Mom just grimaced and said something like "Oh, gosh," and patched up the injury with whatever she had on hand.

There were times when we didn't have either a bandage or tape in the house. In that case, Mom got out a clean old sheet or some piece of cloth, tore off a strip and wrapped up the wounded part. Off we went toward the next adventure wearing our new cloth badge of courage. Mom didn't drive so she either applied first aid or waited for Dad to come home.

-Chapter 27-
Feeding Cattle and Chasing Strays

The main winter job that took all our spare time was feeding the cattle. We had around 100 head of beef cattle out of which we sold 30 or 40 calves and steers in the late fall. During the winter, we fed the livestock by throwing the hay out of the barn into the barnyard. Then, we carried the hay and spread it around with a pitchfork so all the cows could eat. If you didn't spread the hay, the bigger, meaner cows would control the hay and wouldn't let the others eat.

We also had to keep up with the stray cattle and horses. Everyone grazed their cattle on the open range, so each year when our cattle were rounded-up or came in on their own, strays came with them. We'd chase all the livestock into a corral, and by checking the brands, sort out the strays, load them into the truck and haul them back to their owners.

That didn't work for horses whose owners turned them out in the winter to find their own food. If those horses went down by the river, they could usually find some food. In an ideal world, that is how it is supposed to work; but hungry, stray horses always showed up every winter at our place.

The horses ran through our cows, sometimes knocking them down. They also bit and kicked the cows, trying to get at the hay. Sometimes, upset cows lost the calves they were carrying. During deep snow years, we waged a full scale war against stray horses.

Our old dog Tex tried to chase the strays away, but it was a losing battle. Tex bit a mouthful of horsetail hair and even swung on it. Of course, the horses didn't like that and would try to kick him away, but he managed to dodge their kicks. By the time we all got back to the house, those stray horses were back, too.

When the ground was frozen or covered with snow, there was nothing we could throw at them except for frozen horse apples or horse turds. They were about the right size, and if several were frozen together, they were pretty heavy and could hurt a little.

One day, we were all down feeding the cows and had chased the stray horses away, but they'd come back as usual. Old Buck, a big old buckskin horse, was particularly hard to chase away. With Mom on one side, we chased the horses up the road towards the house. Suddenly, they cut around, heading for Mom. Luckily, she was armed with a huge horse apple. She threw it at the horses, and hit one right by the ear. Down he went, knocked out cold!

The snow was flying, and horses were running, but Mom got one good! What a throw! She ruled the barnyard that day. We kids threw many things at those horses, but Mom is the only person I have ever known to have knocked one out with a frozen horse apple.

As I said, we usually lost the battle of the strays. On school days, those clever horses knew that we had to get to school, so they out-waited us and came back as soon as we left for the day.

When summer rolled around, we caught Buck and rode him. He was a big, old work horse as gentle as any kid's horse, but when the snow hit the ground, he became our stray horse enemy number one. You could say we had split feelings towards that old horse.

Feeding cattle in the winter. Note horses outside the fence. (*Wynecoop photo*)

-Chapter 28-
Sled Riding

On weekends and evenings after the chores were done, we got out the old sleds and coasted down the road. We had two well-used sleds that we wanted to play with all day and all night, too, if we could have. But like most kids, we knew that we had chores to do first. So we'd gripe for a while, then do our chores, then have some more fun.

Even though we had store-bought sleds, we enjoyed our homemade versions, too. A large cardboard box was like no other toy. You could roll around in it and slide down the hill a few times before it started breaking up. Once the box broke open, it became a first class toboggan. By simply pulling up the front of the box, you could slide away down the hill.

We also made many of our own sleds by nailing a piece of hard board to the curved back of an old chair. Those modified chairs would really go, but you couldn't steer them, so you just went where they wanted to go.

Our favorite homemade toboggan was made out of corrugated sheet metal that the wind had blown off the barn roof. We bent the nose up a little, but not too far. If it was bent too far as to cause a crease with a sharp edge that cut into the snow, the toboggan didn't work. Once it was fixed and carried to the top of the hill, we would jump on and away we went. There was no way to hold on to this greased lightning, so we usually rolled or bounced off.

That type of toboggan was hard to get back up the hill. Usually we carried it up by putting it on top of our heads, heaving and hauling all the way. We never owned a store-bought toboggan. But, once you had a track started, you could get a good fast ride in the soft snow with that old galvanized roofing material.

In 1947 or 1948, Dad bought a 16mm movie camera and started taking lots of home movies of us. One winter day, he was standing at the bottom of an icy hill waiting for an action scene. We loaded up the old galvanized roofing toboggan, and away we went, zooming down the hill.

Dad was watching us through the camera lens. We started yelling, "Look out! Here we come! Duck, Dad! We're going to hit you!" Dad just stood there with his camera. Before he realized it, we had crashed into him and he and the camera were buried in the snow.

The movie he took shows us speeding down the hill, then the hillside, then trees, then sky, then snow, then nothing. Fortunately, he didn't get hurt. But we had a lot of laughs at his expense.

We always got wet playing outside in the winter. We didn't have waterproof clothing like they have today. To help keep dry, sometimes we wore two pairs of pants and long underwear. Long johns were acceptable for family play, because nobody else would see them. After playing all day in the snow, we were completely soaked through all those layers, so we went in and tried to warm up.

But some winter nights after a fairly warm day, we went down into the field to play on the hard snow crust in the moonlight. It was kind of spooky then. With the moon shining on the snow and ice, it seemed as bright as day. It was a special time, often filled with telling ghost stories from the *Old Ranger* radio program.

-Chapter 29-
Walt's White Thing and Other Scary Stuff

One story, "Walt's White-Thing" was a favorite *Old Ranger* episode. It was about the half-coyote that had haunted the storyteller. The storyteller told about how Walt had tried to shoot the creature, but his gun would not fire. When he took his weapon inside the house to clean it, the cursed gun "accidentally" went off and killed poor Walt. Every time we told the story it seemed more real.

As the storyteller got into it, we'd look around to make sure that the cursed coyote wasn't near by. I always suspected that the White-Thing was closing in on us, because my hair would stand up and a slight chill would creep over me while I listened to the tale.

One night playing in the moonlit field we saw something spooky in the field and we really looked it over. Judge kept whispering: "Its Walt's White-Thing! See, it's only half-dog." The longer we stared at it, the surer we were that it was a ghost. It went down and across the field, then it disappeared.

I can still see that thing in my mind, and I'm not sure what it was. We headed for home FAST and almost convinced the folks that we had really seen Walt's White-Thing this time.

This creepy-chilly feeling was especially strong when we walked our friend, Jim, who lived a couple miles away, part-way home. That really was a scary walk on a full moon night, because along the way there was a big rock that took on the appearance of a face. We called it the "Ghost Rock."

We never noticed that rock during the daytime, but once Jim kept talking about it, our imagination and the Old Ranger's ghost stories took over. From then on, we would do anything to get around that rock – even if it meant walking an extra mile on the new road.

If we were feeling especially brave, we went right up to that rock for the excitement of it all. We knew it was just a rock, but if we watched it long enough, it seemed to move.

Once any one of us thought it had moved, everyone thought it had moved, and down the road we ran. I finally got a good multi-celled flashlight one Christmas, and when I shined it on the rock, the ghost went away. Later on, someone pushed the rock out into the woods with a tractor and we felt safer on our night walks. Until then, that old Ghost Rock could really make the hair on your neck stand up. I have always felt sad about losing the thrill of the Ghost Rock. Too bad it's not there anymore.

Innocent Bible school kids in front of the preacher's haunted house. *(Wynecoop photo)*

There was more spooky neighborhood stuff we had to deal with, including several old haunted buildings. One was the empty Presbyterian minister's house. When it was unoccupied, we figured it had to be haunted. The other spooky house was the old government house up on the hill close to Sonny Campbell's house. Between the two houses was a big old barn that we nosed around. Only a few pigeons lived there behind closed doors.

We also explored the old government barn and warehouses by the Agency. These buildings were usually locked up tight. The weight scales building and blacksmith's shop were seldom used or locked, so we got inside of them a few times and had some fun. It was fun to play blacksmith. I turned the handle on the forge and pretended to heat and bend a metal piece or shaped a horseshoe. Several of the buildings were totally empty. Naturally, we thought all of these empty old buildings might be haunted.

The warehouses were used, especially during the summer. All of the tools for fighting forest fires were stored in them. They were a real treasure chest that we kids never got to explore.

The old barn by Sonny's was huge and sat near his house, across the road from the Presbyterian church. We went over to the barn and looked around, but the big doors were always closed. There were several buildings like that around the neighborhood, empty, not used, and therefore suspected to be haunted. But the big old house next to the barn was considered by ALL of us to be haunted. It sat up high on a raised stone foundation.

For years, we had heard rumors about how some crazy man had stayed in a dungeon in the basement. The house had once been an Indian school and then a jail. Of course, that unusual history attracted kids like iron filings to a magnet.

A screened-in porch on the back of the house had an open door, but the main door to the house was locked. Eventually, some unknown explorer had broken a window in the back door. Once we found it, we crawled into the house and looked around. There was nothing interesting on the main floor, just squeaky doors like on the radio program *Inner Sanctum*.

Of course, we had to make good use of the supposedly scary surroundings, so we started telling ghost stories. That spooked us, so we ran out. After overcoming our fears, we eventually made it back inside. We even mustered enough courage to go down into the basement. There was no dungeon filled with a crazy-man's bones – just an empty, dirty basement. But it was sure exciting when we thought ghosts lived there.

After Mose's house burned down, he and his family moved into this "unhaunted" house. One day, Dick, Steve and I went up to get Richard Phillips to play with us. We were up on the hill behind the house, and as we started down to it, the back screen door flew open and a woman came running out.

Since we were sitting down we just leaned over and down we went into the tall grass, hiding to see what would happen next. She ran towards us and suddenly turned around. Down went her underpants. She went to the bathroom right in front of us. We were in shock. When she finished, up her pants went, and she went back into the house.

I don't think she saw us, or at least she didn't act like it. When that back door shut behind her, there were three of the fastest kids in the west running up that hill into the trees. That was worse than any ghost story.

-Chapter 30-
Ice Skating

Dark nights brought fear of the unknown, but we also managed to have a lot of fun. As we kids got older, we took up ice skating. In the spring, or after a nice warm Chinook wind and rain, ponds formed in the field below the house. Then we waited for the next freeze. That meant good clean ice, no snow to shovel.

In the fall, once the large ponds had frozen, we'd grab a pair of fit-all ice skates and head for the pond. We played tag and "crack the whip" and just glided around on the ice for hours on end.

One winter day when we were down in the field skating, our cousin Ron Brown was with us. It was really getting cold and we wanted to make a fire to warm up. We just couldn't get the fire going, so Ronnie said he would start the fire. He sat down on a piece of wood, took off his socks, and set them on fire. That started the fire okay, but to no one's surprise, Ronnie had cold feet on the long walk home.

Most of the ponds we learned to skate on were really small. I first skated on a pond about the size of two desks. As we became better skaters, we wanted to try bigger ice skating spots. When Wig was old enough, he started driving the old Reo truck. That's when we filled the back full of hay and us kids and started checking out some of the larger shallow lakes. They made for great skating, especially after the first hard freeze in the fall.

There, the ice was clear and free of snow, so we could really play. We always built a big fire. Then, if we could find an old tire, we rolled it into the blaze and let it burn. The black smoke rolled up into the night sky, and we skated in the smoky firelight or moonlight.

With the first freeze, ice on the small shallow lakes popped and cracked when you walked on it. As you zoomed down the ice, you would make a sound that only those who skated on thin ice on a shallow lake would know. It was as if you were skating on a drum, yet different. With each stroke and glide, you'd hear a very clear *vroom-vroom*. But when a lot of skaters were making too much other noise, that particular sound was lost in the commotion. Sometimes the first person on the ice created a crack that followed him across the ice, tracing his path.

Before skating, we always checked the ice with an ax to be sure it was thick enough to skate on. Three inches of ice was the minimum we needed for safety's sake. We wanted even more thickness, but you couldn't wait long because more cold weather usually meant piled-up snow, too.

The good ice skating ended after the first heavy snow. We tried to shovel the snow, and made different kinds of snow plows like a *V*, an angled board, and even used galvanized roofing, but it was no use. We usually gave up on plowing the snow off the ice and checked out other ponds to see if they had clear ice.

Once, when Wig was driving us around in Dad's International pickup in search of frozen ponds, we found what looked like a perfect skating spot. We stopped and all jumped out and ran over to it. Of course, the oldest of us exercised his power and made us wait until he checked the thickness of the ice. We all stood on the bank while he messed around, keeping us in suspense.

That time, we didn't have an ax, but Wig found in the truck a small crowbar that Dad had just bought. Wig finally went onto the ice with Dad's new crowbar. He hit the ice with it, but the ice didn't crack. Then he threw the bar at the ice. *Thunk!* It was gone. It disappeared right through the ice. I don't think Dad ever knew what happened to his new crowbar, but at least we found out that the ice was too thin for skating.

Almost every winter weekend, and some evenings, we went skating, with the exception of basketball season. The coaches didn't want us to skate then because it was hard on our ankles. The folks bought several pairs of skates and we had some others given to us. Since none of our friends took their skates home, there was usually a big tangled pile of blades and laces on the front porch. If the owner didn't show up, his skates were fair game for anyone to use. That way, many kids learned to skate without ever owning a pair of skates. The pile was simply moved out of the way until the next fall.

We occasionally sharpened the blades on our skates, but dull skates were the rule, not the exception. If the skates were too big, the skater used the sides of the blade more than the bottom.

We seldom skated on the big lakes because the folks didn't want us to. But sometimes we couldn't help ourselves. They were fun to skate on, because they had cattails and tules around the edge. On those big lakes we skated faster and built up speed until we crashed into the tules and went tumbling end-over-end. Tules burned well, so we had many a roaring tule fire – especially when the wind blew hard.

We also played a lot of hockey on the bigger ponds. There weren't enough good skaters for us to have much of a game, and we didn't know the rules, so we just made up our own. Anyway, we had a lot of fun with a crooked stick chasing a horse biscuit or a piece of wood around on the ice.

Our homemade hockey sticks were heavy and clubby. We spent more time looking for them, cutting them down, and trying to shape them than we did playing with them. Because it took us so long to make our equipment, we didn't ever play as much hockey as we would have liked. Combine that with wearing skates that were too big, even padded with three pair of Dad's socks, it usually wasn't long before we moved onto some other kind of play. Later on, Dad bought us real hockey sticks and a puck, but looking back, I think our makeshift hockey games were much more fun.

-Chapter 31-
Winter Haystacks

One cloudy, dreary Saturday after we were even older – and supposedly wiser – we went about a mile down into the field to skate on the ponds. In this special play place, there had been a lot of new snow, so skating was out of the question. But since we were down there, we looked around for something else to do.

We decided to check out some neighbors' haystacks down by the trees. The snow was pretty deep, especially to us short-legged kids. As we got closer, we saw that the stacks were covered with snow. We stood there, trying to think of what to do next, getting colder and colder by the minute.

I am not sure if it was the smell of the wild hay or the warmth we thought the hay would provide or, as Red Skelton's "Junior" character would say, "The devil made me do it," but we decided to dig a couple small holes into the bottom of one of the stacks. Although the hay was tightly stacked, we managed to burrow inside. As we'd expected, it was nice and warm there.

Once we warmed up, Wig wanted to get on top of the stack. There was a tall post at the corner of the stack, so he climbed up the post and jumped onto one corner of the top of the haystack. He only crawled around on one corner, and really did little to no damage. I don't think the rest of us followed his fine example, but we probably did. After some time on top, he slid down. We all wandered around a while longer by the stacks, then we headed for home, happy with our new adventure.

Sunday morning we slept in. When we woke up, we could hear two men talking loudly. One was Dad, and we didn't know who the other one was, so at normal curious kids' pace, we jumped out of bed, dressed and ran downstairs.

Dad and a friend sat in the living room talking about something important. We could tell by the visitor's angry tones that this was serious business. We piled onto the couch to get nearer to the action. John B. Flett was complaining about how some kids had ruined his haystacks. They had dug holes into the stacks, been on the top, and just generally wrecked them. Now water would leak into the damaged stacks and ruin the hay.

Uh-Oh! We knew we were in trouble. Rats! No fresh snow had fallen to cover up our tracks. John knew we were guilty, so we had to sit there while the adults determined our punishment. While the judge and jury discussed our fate, we sat listening and shaking on the couch. After hearing their negotiations, which for us was worse than any possible punishment, they agreed that spankings would be fair and just.

Dad stood up and said, "Wig, follow me." They went around the corner out of sight into the hallway. After a short time, we could hear *Whop! Whop! Whop!* Then Wig made a crying sound. That's when the rest of us knew we were dead meat.

Dad came around the corner and said, "Next." Judge got up and followed him into the hallway. Again, the now familiar *Whop! Whop!,* followed by a whimper. Then Judge followed Wig upstairs. Dad came around the corner, and I knew it was my turn. Reluctantly and with great effort, I got off the couch and followed him into the hallway.

Dad could spank really hard, and I was getting ready for the whack when I heard him say, "I will hit my leg, and you cry." I was so surprised! As he hit his leg, I gave it my best effort, but I couldn't do a very good job of crying. When he let me go, I was up the stairs like a shot.

After lying on our beds for a while, we heard a car drive away. Sneaking down to be sure that John had left, We all started celebrating.

But we didn't get off that easy; Dad scolded us about damaging other people's property. We did learn a valuable lesson, though – that our Dad was a fair and compassionate man. We certainly appreciated him for sparing us from spankings that day. We were not an overly emotional family, but at times we did get carried away. A lot of laughing and joking followed our great sighs of relief.

We also learned another lesson well and never touched another person's property after that. If something wasn't ours, we learned to leave it alone.

-Chapter 32-
Sleepwalking

There was no heat upstairs in our new house, so it was real cold in our bedrooms in the winter. Since the old outhouse was mighty far away, we sneaked a can into the bedroom for emergencies. Somehow, there were a lot of emergencies.

We had plenty of blankets to warm us up, but once in a while we all crawled into the same bed. On "two dog nights," Tex and Tim jumped in with us. What fun – with five kids and two dogs in one bed!

I always felt sorry for the one at the bottom of the bed. The one with the roughest soles on their feet usually ended up with the most space. Five or six kids and two dogs sticking out of a bed must have really been a sight to see.

Wig considered himself to be the family singer, and he'd sing to us in bed. He usually tried to sing the current hits, but singing wasn't his best talent. But it was probably the only way he could get us to be quiet and go to sleep.

We usually slept two to a double bed. Dick and Judge normally slept together. They were the sleepwalkers, although once Steve and Dave were found wandering around outside, sound asleep. For some strange reason, most of the sleepwalking was done during the winter months.

At least it was obvious when some of us kids were AWOL from our beds. There was a heat register at the bottom of the stairs, and if the downstairs door was open, some of that heat drifted upstairs. That was our clue that the sleepwalkers were at it again.

The nightwalker's favorite trick was to get out of bed carrying his blankets and go downstairs and sit on the register. After he warmed up, he went back up to bed and left his blankets down on the register. Later, he woke up in bed half-frozen, looking for his missing blankets. This was especially annoying, since he'd wake everyone up, asking for his missing blankets.

We never knew when or if Dick or Judge did the sleepwalking. In the winter, the coldest one went to find blankets. We knew for sure Dick dove – or fell – down the stairs more than once. He didn't get hurt, but he was probably the blanket thief for that night.

Judge explaining a two-dog night to Tim (the dog), while Flash, the other dog, listens. *(Photo courtesy Phoebe Wynecoop)*

-Chapter 33-
Playing in the House

Most of our inside games were played downstairs, since that was the warmest part of the house during the cold months.

One of the growing-up rituals in our family was being able to touch the low wall that hung down from the ceiling between the dining and living room. When I was small, I'd run and jump trying to touch that part of the wall, but I just couldn't make it. Wig and Judge could, but not me. Eventually, my time came, and I could jump and touch it. Then it was no longer a big deal to me. But to the younger ones, it was still a big deal, and they tried to do the same thing until they, too, mastered running and jumping to touch that wall.

We also played knee football in the living room. We usually played two to a side, and used a roll of socks or gloves stuck inside each other for a football. One important rule change from regular football was that you couldn't stand up. You had to run on your knees. That was pretty tough on our knees, especially since we always played tackle. A touchdown was scored on the couch at one end of the room and on a chair at the other. I don't know if we ever scored a touchdown, but we had a lot of fun trying. We broke a few light bulbs and lamps, and that old fir floor without a carpet really made for hard running on the knees and even harder landings everywhere else.

When it was freshly waxed, that floor was really slick. We'd lie on our backs with our butts against the wall and our feet even higher on the wall. If we pushed off real hard, we could slide all the way across the room. This was another game that helped us ruin our clothes. Mom was really happy about that!

We also played a lot of board games. Of course, there was the ever-popular Bingo. We spent many a night playing Bingo. We also learned to play poker and a variety of solitaire card games.

On warm evenings we'd play games upstairs. Slinkies were a lot of fun.

As they worked their way down the stairs, we watched their every move.

Then there were the ghost games. Somewhere, somehow we had acquired a roll of tape that glowed in the dark. We cut out eyes and claws from the tape, then stood next to a light, so the cutouts shined in the dark. After these careful preparations, someone went upstairs wearing the cutouts in the pitch dark.

Once he was ready and waiting, the rest of us would sneak cautiously up the stairs. The shiny eyes and claws would jump out and scare us almost to death. We all knew the glowing monster lurked up there somewhere, but we were still terrified when it surprised us. Sometimes even the ghost got scared and ran with the others.

We learned how to make a fast exit down the stairs to escape from the monster. First you sat down on the top stair. Then you straightened your legs, picked your seat up, and leaned back like you were standing tall. *Whoosh!* You just shot down the stairs like a piece of lumber going down the chute. It was hard to stop at the bottom, but at least you got away from the monster – FAST.

There was only one light in the upstairs hall, and it was turned on with a pull string. After an evening of playing ghost downstairs, no one wanted to go upstairs to pull on the light. So we waited around until several of us wanted to go to bed badly enough, then we would all go up in a tight group to do the honors. The light usually didn't work, making it harder to go to bed.

As we grew older, we still liked to listen to the radio. *Captain Midnight*, *Gang Busters*, *Don Winslow of the Coast Guard*, and the news were our favorite programs. I remember hearing the radio news of President Roosevelt's death and about the end of World War II in Europe and in the Pacific.

Boxing was another favorite kind of indoor play. Dad always talked about his brief career as a boxer and what a good sport boxing was. He seldom played any kind of ball with us, but he took the time to teach us how to box. He bought several pairs of boxing gloves, and he gave us boxing

**Dick and Dave in 1939. Dave may have been the youngest boxer
on the Reservation.** *(Photo courtesy Phoebe Wynecoop)*

lessons. Unfortunately, not one of us wanted to be a boxer. Still, we listened to all the big-time boxing matches on the radio. The announcer made the matches so exciting! We rooted for our favorite contender like all of the adults did.

After World War II ended, Uncle Glenn came to our house to visit, and he liked to sing songs about Alaska. He wasn't the best singer, nor was he the worst. We wound up his arm like an old phonograph and he'd sing his favorite song,

Dad, Judge and Wig duking it out. *(Photo courtesy Phoebe Wynecoop)*

Squaws Along the Yukon. I'm surprised we didn't wear him out – or at least cripple his arm, with all that cranking.

Our dogs Tim and Tex, later Ike and Nixon, didn't escape from our games. We'd sneak some clothes downstairs and/or take the dogs upstairs and dress them. That was always worth a laugh! Old Tex and his shaggy hair really looked neat with pants and a shirt on. We never ran out of fun things to do indoors.

Ike dressed for the day. *(Wynecoop photo)*

-Chapter 34-
Construction Projects

As I mentioned earlier, we always walked to school. The trail went from our back door, up the hill, across our toboggan track, across the creek, through a swamp, past an apple orchard, up to the road, and then to the school. We followed this same trail to both Sunday School and public school.

Crossing the creek and swamp was really tough. To do that, we walked on downed trees or threw limbs into the mud, making a very poor bridge. We still ended up with wet feet going to and from our destination.

To improve on that unfortunate situation, we decided to build a real bridge. We put two logs across the creek bed, then we nailed boards onto the logs. That made a pretty neat bridge. There was still a mud hole at one end where it was easy to fall into the water, but at least our flimsy bridge was a big improvement. We used it for several years, but when the logs rotted out we were back to square one.

Our next effort was to build another bridge about four feet higher than the creek. For this, we nailed boards to trees on each end and put logs on the boards. Then, we once again nailed the platform boards to the support logs. Next, we built a short ramp on one end. We also made a short addition to the other end of the high bridge with its own long ramp. Finally, we added handrails to both sides of the structure. We had built a bridge any engineer would have been proud of. That bridge was real solid and lasted until we found a new route to school.

On hot summer days, it was nice and cool in the trees down by the creek, so we spent a lot of time playing there. Since the stinging nettles were really thick and tall, we made swords out of sticks and mowed the nettles down so we could walk through the place without being stung. Once, while exploring along the creek, Dave found an old grinding rock made of granite that had been used by people years ago, probably the local tribe. At some point in time, that old grinding rock disappeared, like a lot of other things that might have been valuable to somebody today.

Well, our construction projects didn't stop there. Our eyes were soon attracted to several clumps of quaking aspen growing near our bridge. Judge and Dick nailed steps up the trunks of two trees to a point that was relatively square. Then they nailed two other boards to the aspen and more boards to the top of the first two boards, which gave them the floor for a tree house.

One floor was not enough! We added second and third floors. Those upper floors didn't work out because the trees swayed too much on windy days and the nails pulled out. Since the top floors always had to be re-nailed, we finally gave up on maintaining them. Judge and Dick were the main tree-house builders.

Picket fence gate project, with the garage in the background. *(Wynecoop photo)*

We had other tree houses, too. Along the road leading down to the house, we cut out the top of a fir tree for a Christmas tree and nailed a seat on the top of the remaining trunk. That was a good tree house for one person. There was a seat and a footrest, but it was hard to get up onto that perch. Once on the seat, you swayed around in the wind like an acrobat in a circus. What a ride!

We also had a pine tree that we cut the top out of for a tree house. It was not as good as the fir, because it didn't sway around much, and swaying was a major part of the fun.

As you can imagine, there were never many loose boards lying around our place, since we always added them to our bridges or tree houses or some other building project. Lumber was the limiting factor in most of our construction work. We could have kept a sawmill busy supplying us with materials.

-Chapter 35-
Bible School

Public school was not the only school we attended. In the summer we went to Bible School. That was a one week class, usually in June. We played games, sang songs and did some Bible class work. There were a lot of kids present, so it was a fun session. The Catholic kids had their catechism class at the same time, and we occasionally crossed paths. We played softball several times. It was strange, because at public school we were all good friends, essentially the same, but the church schools separated us. There were a lot of Presbyterians, so we had a lot of fun.

Bible school attendees with Campbell's house on the left and the Presbyterian Church on the right. Some of the kids and adults in the photo are: George Wynne, Mr. & Mrs. Lee, Buckshot Sherwood, Robert Sherwood, Jean Campbell, Wig Wynecoop, Midge Tandy, Martha Flett, Anne Flett, Chick Wynecoop, Sonny Campbell, Willy Boyd, Ruth Galbraith, Dorothy Wynne, Squeak Tandy, Carson Sherwood, Dave Wynecoop, Steve Wynecoop, Johnny Wynne, Everett Tandy, Dick Wynecoop, Chuck Cox, Judge Wynecoop, Viola Cox, Esther Lowley and Richard Phillips. *(Wynecoop photo)*

When Mr. Lee was the minister, he set up several youth groups, where we were divided up by age, and each group did various activities such as reading the Bible and studying what the reading meant. We were told that at the end of one of the classes we would each have to say a prayer. That caused me some real heartburn. Praying was the preacher's job and not mine. I drug it out as long as I could, avoiding leading a prayer, until there was no one left except me. I had thought this through pretty carefully and started with "please bow your head" and then said, "We will now have a silent prayer." No one said a word. I waited a while, and then said "Amen." It worked, but that set up a barrier for me and I slowly quit going to church. I now attend church regularly, but I still am not a leader when it's time to pray.

More Bible school kids. *(Wynecoop photo)*

-Chapter 36-
The Milk Cow

We seemed to find time for construction projects in the spring or early summer, but we still had our regular chores to do. When the grass was fresh, the old milk cow would go her own way in search of food. She had a bell on a belt around her neck, but that didn't stop her wandering far and wide as she looked for greener grass.

On school days, when she took off in search of better feed, we had to find her both before and after school. Once, I found her way up on the hill, but she usually wandered down into the field below.

One evening, I found her way down in the field. As I started chasing her home, I remembered how our dog Tex had swung on cows' and horses' tails, so I thought, "Why not give it a try?" I grabbed her dirty tail and it was really yucky, but I held on. She didn't seem to mind much, so as we went along, I became a little braver. I started to swing and then bounced up and down, hanging on and having fun. She looked around and acted like she didn't like that at all.

Suddenly, she huffed real loud and a stream of cow manure came out and nailed me right in the stomach. What a mess! Stinky, runny cow manure plastered me all over! I guess she thought I had it coming. Luckily, I had to cross the creek, so I was able to get most of it off with a stick and some water. I didn't ever swing on her tail again.

Dick actually rode the old milk cow and even managed to get a saddle on her several times. She didn't react in a bad way to being ridden like she did when I was swinging on her tail. Maybe it was personal. She didn't seem to like me very much.

Of course, we fed this cow a special diet designed to increase her milk production. She often ate oats and Bran-an-shorts, a commercial cattle feed. Having good quality milk was important to us, so we fed "Jingle" well.

Since Dick and Judge did most of the milking, I was usually just a substitute. I quickly learned that short fingernails were very necessary for that job. As the milker, I had to sit right next to the cow and put my head against her flank in front of her hind leg. This let her know what was going to happen.

Since we usually set the bucket on the ground, I had to throw away many a bucket of milk because she'd halfway kick and step into the bucket. Her hoof was usually covered with manure, so when she did this, the bucket of milk was spoiled.

The worst thing about milking was to be slapped on the head by a nasty tail soaked with manure and urine. To keep that from happening, I usually tied the tail to something. That was the only way to keep her out of my hair!

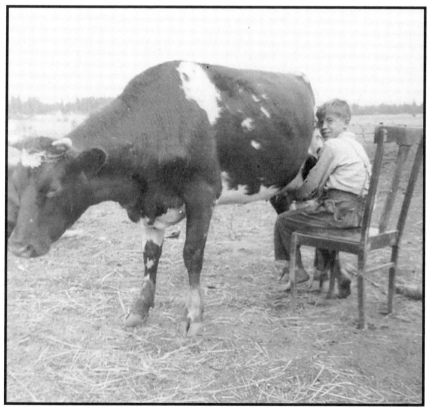

Judge milking the cow. *(Photo courtesy Phoebe Wynecoop)*

Milking operation. From left: Chick, Dick (holding a banty chicken), Judge, Steve and Tim, the dog. *(Photo courtesy Phoebe Wynecoop)*

-Chapter 37-
Riding Horses

Our first horse riding was on stick horses, and we took great pride in those bony mounts. Since real horses had metal shoes, we decided to make some for ourselves for special effects. To make our horseshoes, we carefully stomped on a condensed milk can or some other can that did not have the top cut out. If you positioned the stomp just right, the can bent up around the heel of your shoe. Then we went clomping around, riding our stick horses and sounding real authentic in our metal horseshoes, *clippety-clop, clippety-clop!*

We may have stretched our limits when we brought our stick horses into the house, tied them up in the hallway and brought in hay and water for them, but Mom didn't seem to mind. Eventually, we moved on to riding real horses.

We did our fair share of horse riding, but we probably would have done a lot more if we could have caught the horses better. That was hard to do. Those free spirits knew every trick in the book to evade us. We could get close to pet them, but when we tried to catch them to ride, forget it.

We learned to lure them into the corral by feeding them oats in a bucket. Sometimes we just teased them with an empty bucket. That usually worked to get them inside the corral, but then they still wanted to see what was inside of the bucket. Horses will do anything for any type of grain, especially oats. After they were inside the corral, we closed the gate.

Our favorite horse was Champ, a nice black gelding. He was a good kid's horse, and we all rode him, but he was considered to be Judge's horse. Champ put up with a lot of dumb things from us. One day he was lying down comfortably in the field, just resting. For some reason, I had to ride him, so I went over to start chasing him into the corral. As I got close to Champ, I expected him to jump up and run, but he just lay there on his side.

He was sound asleep – probably dreaming horse dreams. I walked right up to him, but he still didn't move. I was carrying a bridle, so I carefully tied the reins around his neck, but I didn't put the bridle on, walked around in front of him, then went to his left side. I jumped on his back. That woke him. Up he jumped, and instead of bucking or running, he just stood there.

Then he looked around at me, looked forward, then turned around and looked again. He could not figure out how I had been able to catch him, let alone tie the reins around his neck while he was down and out.

With a lot of practice and persistence, we were able to catch the horses and ride them, but there was an important middle step that was the downfall of both us kids and horses, too. That was getting up onto the horse.

Since we usually rode bareback, there was no stirrup or saddle horn to hold on to. One method was to crawl up the horse's leg and then try to grab a handful of mane. If that didn't work, you led the horse next to a

Scruffy little Steve and his teddy bear watching his brother, "Handsome Chick" cleverly out-wrangle a horse.

fence or a piece of equipment or a stump or anything that would give you the height to jump onto its back without going over the other side.

One problem was that you might be able to get your horse next to the fence, but by the time you climbed the fence, the horse would step sideways and be too far away for you to jump onto it. This would go on over and over until you finally got on or someone came to help. This was one of our lessons on how to be patient and to keep trying, no matter how frustrating a situation might be.

It seemed like the only time the horse cooperated and stood next to you was when he was standing on your foot. That really hurt. Luckily, the ground was usually soft and the horses were not shod, so no foot bones were broken.

Riding bareback took some special skill. By leaning back and sticking your legs forward for balance or by letting them hang loose at the sides, you could ride bareback at a gallop or run without much trouble. Trotting was the killer, because you bounced all over the place, especially from side to side.

Riding bareback was one thing, but riding double bareback was something else altogether and not to be taken lightly. When riding double, you can't lean back – you have to ride straight up or suffer the consequences.

Since we didn't own or need enough horses for everyone to have his own horse, we rode double a lot. I usually rode any horse that was available. Sometimes I even put a bridle on one of the stray horses that always seemed to be hanging around, taking my chances on how it would behave.

Once, down in the field, Judge was riding bareback and I was walking. Together, we were chasing the other horses back towards the barn. It usually took more than one person to round up the horses and chase them into the corral.

That time, the horses we were after were lined out pretty well and were trotting towards the barn, all according to plan. Judge stopped his horse and held out his foot, so I was able to step on it and swing up behind him. Away we went, riding double bareback.

Most horses are a little sway-backed, and as the horse trots along, double bareback riders are forced together by the natural curve of the horse's back. When the horse trots, the two riders start bouncing until they are almost glued together. The back rider has to hold on tightly to the front rider or he might fall off. As long as you bounce together and stay centered on the horse, everything's okay.

But remember, in real life nothing works A-okay, especially when two kids are riding bareback. First, we started bouncing high, then we started bouncing to the side. Judge righted himself and our problem by grabbing a hank of horse mane. This worked for a short while.

We two riders now bounced along completely out of control, which meant that now four legs were hitting the poor horse. Judge griped about my being too close, and told me to slide back. "Yea, sure!" I grumbled. I tried to slide back for one gallop, but then we were stuck back together.

When the horse is going in a straight line, you can usually enjoy the ride with no major problem. But all it takes is for the horse to make a little change in direction, and you are off center and then leaning too far to the side. Champ stepped wide, changing direction, and the next thing we knew, we were both lying on the ground, coughing and choking in the dust, hoping no one had seen us fall off.

I think we jumped up almost before we hit the dirt. But that sudden jolt was pretty rough. Except for a major loss of pride, we were okay, but very dirty and much wiser. We went on to the barn with only one person riding the horse. The reader can speculate who it was.

Riding bareback was fun, but after a while you smelled like a horse because your pants got soaked with horse sweat. Still, riding with a blanket and no saddle was even worse. That blanket just added something else to slip and slide around on and increased your odds of falling off.

One time, I caught Champ and wanted to ride him to the house from the corral, but I had forgotten to bring a bridle. Somewhere I had heard that the old Indians just tied a long string around the horse's lower jaw and didn't use a bridle. Well, to me that was worth a try.

There was some twine nearby, so I tied one piece of it loosely around Champ's lower jaw. He didn't seem to mind, so I led him over to the corral. After several attempts, I was able to mount him.

We went over to the corral gate, opened it and headed up the road. I jumped off and led him through the other gate and got back on and was thinking, "This is working out okay." Champ started an easy gallop, and I leaned back and had some fun. Then Champ went even faster, knowing there were oats in the garage. I pulled on the ends of the strings, but I was pulling back on air. The twine had come loose.

By then, we were going pretty fast, but at least we were headed in the right direction. I was riding bareback so I grabbed a hunk of mane and went along for the ride.

By now, Champ was running completely loose, and I was hanging on real tight. When we slowed to make the corner onto the road to the house, I knew I'd be okay. Champ slowed down and trotted down to the house, then stopped by the picket fence gate. Judge put a rope on him and Champ acted as if nothing happened. That was my first and last time riding a horse bridle-less, Indian style.

Another time, Wig, Judge and I had a good adventure down in the canyon. Wig was riding Champ, complete with a saddle and bridle, which he usually insisted on. That was not the mode for Judge and me, for a couple reasons.

When we were small, we couldn't get the bridle on a horse, because the horse would raise his head too high for us to reach. Or sometimes the horse wouldn't open its mouth so we could put the bit inside. And a saddle was too heavy for us to carry, let alone put on top of a horse.

Anyway, we were branching out into new territory down in the canyon where we usually didn't go, following the old logging railroad track. Our dog Tex was with us; we never went far without him. Tex started barking ahead of us, and when we caught up with him, we saw what had gotten him so excited. A big old diamondback rattlesnake was coiled up alongside the road. That snake didn't survive our assault – a hail of rock and clubs. Soon we had a trophy rattle that measured about 2 inches long. That snake was as big around as my arm and as long as I was tall.

Once you kill a rattlesnake with a dog present, if you're sneaky, you can reach down and tap the dog on the leg and he'll really jump and growl. Poor old Tex was a nervous wreck by the time we got home. The first time we pinched him, he must have jumped ten feet and let out a high-pitched yelp. We really laughed, but it didn't seem fair to scare our best four-legged friend too much.

Down the road from where we had killed the snake lived a couple we didn't know, whose names were Wood and Katherine Lanham. With our good imaginations, we figured that Wood was probably more dangerous than the rattlesnake. We'd heard stories about him, and we didn't trust him at all. Wood was supposed to be mean, and he had one bad eye, so he was automatically to be feared. As we approached the couple's house, we all crawled onto Champ. Judge sat in front of the saddle. Wig rode in the saddle. I brought up the rear, perching behind the saddle.

The Lanhams' white house was off to one side of the road. We went roaring down the last bit of the old railroad bed, then up their road to the main road. We thought that we'd escaped from a desperate predicament again! From what? That's hard to explain, because there was really nothing to run from! In later years, we came to know the mysterious Lanhams well, and they became great family friends.

That was the only time I remember riding triple, which was really risky, but at the time, it seemed to be a life-or-death absolute necessity. I am surprised one of us didn't fall off. We were really moving out, and more than excited, so anything could have happened.

Shortly after all our adventures with Champ, he was hit by a car and had to be put away. That was a shame, because he was a good riding horse. Champ's claim to fame was his ability to avoid getting caught too quickly. After we yelled at him many times, he let us catch him eventually, and then he was fun to ride. He did everything at kid speed, not too fast, and he tolerated us kids really well.

We missed him a lot after he was gone.

Horses were always a big part of our lives. The horse in this photo is April. Her riders are Dick, Steve and Dave. *(Photo courtesy Phoebe Wynecoop)*

-Chapter 38-
Playing with Friends

We spent a lot of time riding bicycles. At that time, there was only one kind of bike, one with no gears and a rear wheel brake. A Schwinn bike with a light was the top-of-the-line.

In those days, there were no training wheels to help you learn how to ride. You simply crawled on the bike while someone steadied it, then with a push, away you went. After many crashes, you finally mastered the old bike and joined the rest of the bike riders.

I never owned a bike, but there were always enough around that one would be available to me. My friend Sonny's folks wouldn't let him ride a horse, but we sure had fun on our bicycles.

Our main summertime bicycle adventures involved collecting beer and pop bottles. We seldom just rode our bikes around for nothing. We always had to have a reason. Earning a penny a bottle for beer bottles and two to five cents for pop bottles were good reasons.

In our spare time, we covered the roads looking for empty bottles. We put them in a sack or in the basket on Sonny's bike. Loose bottles were hard to handle, so an empty pop or beer case really came in handy for our big hauls.

Once we had a full case, we hid it near an easy place to find, like behind a big tree or rock pile. Then we went on down the road looking for more. When we had picked up all the bottles, Sonny conned his Dad into taking his car out and picking up our stashes for us. When we accumulated a good-sized collection, we'd take them all down to Peterson's Market or to the Ford Store and sell them. Mr. Peterson was a good man who always bought our bottles.

My share of the little money we made came in handy to buy the special treats I thought I needed. Combining my bottle money with my squirrel

Judge and Wig transporting Dick and Dave in a beer box, with Chick behind them. *(Photo courtesy Phoebe Wynecoop)*

trapping money (five cents a tail), I always had extra spending money that allowed me to buy candy. Unfortunately, these sweet treats contributed to my bad teeth and the visits to the much-hated dentist chair.

With some of our extra money, we'd also buy a bottle of pop. I guess you could say those empty pop bottles were turned into tasty filled ones. We drank a lot of creme soda, strawberry or whatever was available. Back then, we didn't have the variety of flavors that are available today. Somehow, we started adding peanuts to some of the soda pops, especially creme soda or Pepsi.

First, you'd drink some of the pop. Then, you'd pour a bag of peanuts into the rest of it. What a drink that made! The last peanuts always stayed in the bottom of the bottle, so you had to swish the pop around and quickly drink it to get the last peanuts into your mouth.

Pop or soda bottles were supposedly cleaned and then refilled. But more than once we found a cigarette butt in the bottle. That was not very appetizing. Those early attempts at recycling were far from perfect.

Our other extra-money treat was ice cream. Each of us bought his own pint or quart, usually strawberry flavored. Then we all ran down the hill below the store and sat on the ground in the trees and ate it – all at once. Nothing was left over for a later time.

Since Sonny and I were good friends, his Mom occasionally invited me over for a drink of water or to play at his house. They had a nice big home, and some strict rules to go with it. I could not go into the living room or touch the living room furniture. I could go up to his room if I took my shoes off, walked around the edge of the carpet to the bottom of the steps, and then went upstairs.

I remember one time when I slipped and stepped on the carpet. Of course, his Mom saw me. I wasn't yelled at or kicked out, but I ran up the stairs really fast to escape her stern look. Sonny called his mom Mother, and this gave her a different status, like she was up on a pedestal. My Mom was always Mom – the way it should be.

Sonny had a lot of games. His real treasure was his comic book collection. He had comic books about all of my radio heroes. Since we were in the same grade in school, we had learned to read together. The hours we spent reading comic books probably helped develop my interest in reading. My cousins Larry and Ronnie Brown also had a pile of comic books, so along with theirs and the ones we had at home, and Sonny's collection, we had plenty of comics to read.

I remember one of our comic books that measured about three inches square and two inches thick. Each page had a normal cartoon on it, but there was also a small picture in the upper right hand corner. When you held the book in your left hand and pressed down with your right thumb and released the pages one-at-a-time, the small pictures came alive. The characters ran, jumped or flew – whatever they were drawn to do. With some imagination, watching these pictures was like watching a movie.

Not many real books were available to us. The only library nearby was the school library, and we were too young to check out books. I didn't know about a public library until I was in college. But we usually received some books for Christmas presents. We also read the magazines that the folks subscribed to, like *True, Outdoor Life and Boys Life.*

We also played pick-up sticks, worked jigsaw puzzles and enjoyed checkers and other games. Sonny had an older sister Jean, who was seldom home. Since she was several years older, the last thing she wanted to do was spend a lot of time playing with all of us boys.

Like Granddad, Sonny even owned a stereoscope – a neat invention for viewing pictures and photographs in stereo. First, you put a card with two pictures on it into a tray several inches from the eye pieces. Then, by positioning the viewer up close to your eyes, you could see the images with added depth. The scenes of wild and exotic places really showed us special sights. These stereoscope pictures were part of the new visual fad that was later known as "3-D."

One Christmas, one of us kids got one of the new viewer models that had the pictures on a disc. We just about wore that thing out looking at the colored pictures, especially the ones from St. Augustine, Florida. There were also cartoon characters and other features on other disks, but to me, the white sands of Florida were the best.

Mom or Dad told us how to make stilts, so naturally we built some to play with. Stilts were made from two long poles to which we nailed a short piece of 2"x4" for a footrest and a leather strap to hold your foot in place.

Mounting those stilts was almost like getting onto a horse. First, you stood on something tall. Then, you stuck your feet into the slot on top of the board and under the strap. The poles were long, usually towering up above your head. By holding the tall poles tightly behind you and up against your side, you could usually stand up and walk around a while. Holding the poles tight against your side was the key to staying upright.

Since stilts were awkward and clumsy, they were a dangerous form of entertainment for us. Judge was the engineer and builder. Dick was the test pilot. The taller the stilts, the more likely you'd be to fall and the farther you had to fall. Falling was bad, because your feet were held in place by the leather straps. If or when you fell down, your first priority was to get your feet free to land on. If you couldn't clear your feet, you were in a twisted heap of trouble.

I can imagine what total strangers thought when they drove down the driveway to our house and saw all of us kids walking around on stilts. Dick's pair stood five or six feet tall, much longer than the normal pair which was more like three to four feet tall.

I remember one nice fall day when one of our friends by the name of Bruce came down to play. We'd all been upstairs playing, but decided to go downstairs. Since the weather was nice, the windows were open. Suddenly, I saw something red flash past the kitchen window. We ran to the window and saw an apple sailing out from an upstairs window. It landed about 20 feet away in the field behind the house.

We ran back upstairs to check things out and found that Bruce (who had come over to play) was throwing apples out the bedroom window. We figured out that he was planning to take them home later. That really surprised us, and our angry Mom sent him home without the apples. Several of us retrieved those apples, but they had been bruised when they landed and were not too good for eating anymore.

Dick walking on short stilts. Dave is on the left. (*Photo courtesy Phoebe Wynecoop)*

Real chicken friends. Top photo, Steve and Dave. Bottom photo, Steve. *(Photos courtesy Phoebe Wynecoop)*

-Chapter 39-
Trapping and Hunting

Ground squirrels just over-ran the meadow below our house. They ate so much grass that it was hardly worth cutting in some places. I caught a lot of them, but never enough to make a dent in their population. My agreement with Dad was for tails. I cut the dead squirrels' tails off and tied them onto a string. When I gave them to Dad, he paid me the agreed-on bounty of five cents each.

I spent many hours checking my trap lines for these pests. The old spring traps had a trigger in between the trap's arms. When the squirrel stepped on the trigger, the trap snapped shut, catching the animal. The trap's long chain was attached to a peg in the ground. This kept the victim from escaping.

I once caught a badger, but it was able to dig itself deep into the ground and I couldn't pull it out. Badgers also hunted the squirrels, and their large holes damaged both our animals and our equipment. If a horse stepped into the hole, it could break a leg, although it never happened to one of our horses. A badger's dirt pile and hole snared and broke several pieces of expensive equipment.

Another time, I caught a skunk in a spring trap. Even though it was dead when I found it, the awful smell was still there. I wanted to show him off, so I dragged him home, but Mom smelled me coming. When I was about halfway there, she ordered me to throw it into a hole and bury it. Skunks can really smell, especially when you're close to them.

When I turned twelve, Dad gave me a Winchester "Model 62" .22 rifle. Since I shot left-handed like he did, he thought a pump model would be better for me to shoot than a right-handed bolt action. He also bought me lots of shells. That's when I graduated to shooting squirrels. I spent many hours down in the field doing just that, and I was able to shoot many more of the pesky varmints than I'd ever been able to trap. I still had the same agreement with Dad for squirrel bounty, a nickel a tail.

Hunting was a great sport for a kid. Of course, certain rules came with the territory. Luckily, there were no houses close by. And I didn't shoot towards the road or distant houses. Most of my shooting was into the ground, not into the air. There were other rules, like never pointing a gun at another human or towards your own feet.

To us kids, guns were more practical tools than toys, but we did learn one dumb and dangerous trick. We tossed live cartridges into a fire, then everyone scattered. After the cartridges exploded, we repeated the process. That made for fun fireworks, but it was an expensive thrill, because I couldn't trade squirrel tails for exploded shells.

When we did this, the bullet didn't travel like it did when it was fired from a rifle. The cartridge case would be split open from the explosion. Everyone thought this was fun but me. I didn't enjoy this much, because I was the only one with an agreement with Dad to shoot squirrels for bounty.

Still, Dad did not want us to throw cartridges into a fire. When he was about our age, he had hit a dynamite cap with a hammer and permanently damaged his right eye. Although he was right-handed, he shot left-handed because of this eye injury. He didn't like for us to take risky chances with guns and live ammo.

We kids were the bird hunters in our family. In the fall, after the hay was put up for the year, we went grouse hunting. One time, Wig and I were hunting with Tex and Tim, our two dogs. Wig was leading the way as we walked along an old road that led to where someone had been cutting cordwood or wood that was split to be used in large stoves. The cordwood sections, generally four feet long and 6-12 inches across, were stacked in a pile to dry at the end of the road.

As we came up to the pile, there was some noise behind it, and Wig yelled, "Rabbits! Let's get them!" Around the pile we ran, and something hit me on the legs, then Wig and the gun were hit. Man, did it stink!

Wig's rabbit was really a skunk, and it had nailed both of us. When you're that close and get sprayed by a skunk, the odor is not like the pungent smell from a distance. It's really beyond putrid and it almost makes you sick. We were in bad shape. I'll bet you could smell us for miles.

We were not far from the house, so we headed home. As we headed down the hill towards the house, Mom was outside and ordered us to stop. We had to dig a hole with a shovel, then take off all of our clothes and bury them. After many days out in the sun, the gun eventually stopped smelling like skunk. Old Tex was in a bad way, but after many baths and days outside, he no longer smelled. Our legs were not too bad and after many washings with good old lye soap, we were okay. That smelly experience ended the grouse hunting season early for us that year.

We could hunt as much as we wanted to, just as long as we stayed within some limits; no body shooting was allowed, and we had to clean everything we brought home. We could not expect Mom to do the skinning or cleaning. Just like with the fish, I always cleaned my edible game; of course, ground squirrels were not considered edible.

Our hunts were usually successful, but we paced ourselves. We often passed up birds so that there would be some to hunt next year. But, as I've said before, we had no mercy on the pesky squirrels.

We even tried hunting with slingshots, which was a little more challenging than hunting with rifles. Our main problem was carrying good slingshot-sized rocks. Our pockets were bulging with so many rocks that we could hardly keep our pants up. Occasionally, we'd nail a bird, but we usually ran out of rocks before we hit anything. We spent a long time practicing with slingshots, and even tried out a sling like the one David had probably used to slay Goliath.

The real problem in making a slingshot was finding real rubber to use for the sling. Back then, all automobile tires had inner tubes, and folks fortunate enough to own a car kept their valuable real-rubber inner tubes.

During the war, the only inner tubes available were made out of synthetic rubber, and these were the only source of rubber for our slings. Flat tires were really common, so inner tubes had patches on the patches, and once a tube was thrown away, there was not much left for slingshots.

Synthetic rubber did not stretch and snap back like real rubber. We could really tell the difference between the two. Real rubber would shoot a rock a considerable distance, while a synthetic rubber slingshot would dribble a rock with no speed or distance or power.

The perfect slingshot required a good forked green-willow handle, so we spent many hours looking for the right willow. Once we found one, we peeled the bark off and cut notches around the two forks. Then we pulled the rubber as tight as possible around one fork. While one person stretched it as far as he could, someone else tied a string around the rubber right next to the notch in the fork. If this wasn't done right, when you pulled the rubber, the strip would come off the fork. So the rubber had to be anchored and stretched real tight.

We tied both forks this way, then at the back end of the rubber strips, we tied on a leather pocket. To do that, first you cut a strip in the leather on opposite sides. Then the rubber strips were inserted into the slit and looped back against itself. Next, holding the leather in one hand and the looped rubber in another, you pulled them as tight as possible. Repeating this with both strips, we had made a fine slingshot.

Green willow was good for other things. For example, I'd cut a smooth 4-5-inch-long piece that was about 3/4 inch across. When I tapped the bark with a stick or knife, it eventually came loose and I could pull it off. Then I notched one end and cut a grove about an inch long near the angled end. When I put the skin or bark back on the twig, I had made a whistle. At least in theory, this was a whistle, but in real life my whistle didn't work very well.

Learning to whistle with our lips was one of our more frustrating ventures. We could all make a whistling noise with our lips, but it was not very loud. We worked many hours trying without success to achieve perfect whistles, both the real shrill two-fingered kind and the regular one.

We spent so many hours trying to get the right technique, puckering our lips and finding the right position of our tongues and lips against our teeth, but to no avail. Ball players could really whistle. And Dad could always blow our ears off with his whistle.

Eventually, Wig and Steve developed the right whistling technique. But, no matter how hard I blew, all I got was a blowing air sound. Wig said, "All you do is curl your tongue against your lower teeth and suck your lip in against your lower teeth and pucker your upper lip and blow." Yea, sure! I blew until I was blue-faced, but not a sound came out. I always envied Dad and my brothers for their baseball-player-quality whistles.

Now, back to our hunting tales. One day while we were at school we heard about a cougar roaming around out near our Aunt Esther's place – she had moved from her house of the radio story. The next Saturday morning, about eight of us got together to go cougar hunting. Armed with a single shot .22 rifle and various clubs, and accompanied by our trusty dogs, we started for Esther's place. She lived about five miles away at the end of the mountain behind our house.

We started bravely up the hill. The snow was only ankle-deep at our house, but it was knee-deep up on top of the hill. Along the way, we made so much noise, that if there had been a cougar around, it would have had plenty of time to disappear before we got anywhere near it.

We trudged on through the snow and eventually got to Aunt Esther's. We knew all about her unfriendly animals. She had an old sheep that would knock you down if you turned your back on it. She also had an aggressive goose. After having been chased by both, we were a little leery of going up too close to her house.

After carefully looking around the yard, we decided that since it was winter, the ornery goose and sheep were probably locked in the barn. We scurried across the yard and into the house before they had a chance to attack.

Aunt Esther was a little more than surprised that we had all walked out there to save her from the cougar. She said she had not seen or heard a cougar and told us that we were wasting our time hunting for one. We finally convinced her that we were safe and would not get eaten by the phantom cougar on our way home. Since there were so many of us, we figured that there was safety in numbers.

There were so many of us that we overran her little house. But we cougar hunters decided to stay just a little while to warm up before heading for home. Aunt Esther did not have electricity, but she had something we liked very much – an old phonograph that had a crank-up handle. Once it was wound and ready, she let us play some of her old records. Our favorite was *Barnacle Bill, the Sailor Man*. That song was really funny and always made us laugh. She also had other records that we had to be very careful with.

After our short visit with Aunt Esther, we left her place and went back up the trail toward home. The trudge back through the snow wasn't filled with the same anticipation and excitement as the trip out had been. We never saw a cougar, but we did have a nice, long walk and enjoyed listening to *Barnacle Bill* and visiting with Aunt Esther again. What we didn't mind not seeing were her mean old sheep and goose.

The Indian Reservation had only a few limited hunting restrictions. As tribal members, we followed the seasons imposed by the Tribal Council. No deer hunting was allowed in the late winter or spring. Our family had its own seasonal rules and regulations: only buck hunting after July 4 and no doe hunting until after September 1.

After the war, our uncles who lived off of the reservation came back to hunt. Every fall, they'd hunt deer, and they usually invited us because we knew the country. They were fun to hunt with, and as we got to know them, we gave them a nickname based on a particular trait they demonstrated. Other folks also noticed peculiar things about our uncles and tried to describe them with nicknames.

Everyone called Uncle Jack Knoll "Coats." This was because he wore so many coats that we were afraid that if he ever fell down, he would never be able to get up again. He was also the school superintendent that I mentioned in an earlier story. We never openly called him by his

Reservation name, but I am sure he knew about it somehow.

Another uncle, Wayne Sutton, we called "Drag-Along." He walked too slow and was always behind everybody else. He was good-natured and fun to tease, and he teased us back all the time too.

Believe it or not, our lives weren't always full of action, so we occasionally had to invent some fun. During one hunting season, we came up with the idea of making a cardboard deer to find out if someone would shoot it. First, we found a large sheet of cardboard and drew on it the outline of a deer. Next, we cut the deer out and nailed several boards to the back of the cardboard. We then selected the site for the fake deer, and drove the boards into the ground to keep it standing tall.

The location we chose was great. It was in the small bushes along a small clearing. It wasn't long before rumors started to fly about someone shooting up our cardboard deer. Sure enough, we found bullet holes in the decoy deer, but were they from someone thinking they were shooting a deer, or from someone shooting it to make us think that? I guess we'll never know for sure.

At a picnic with our uncles. L to R: Chuck Tandy, Glenn Galbraith, Dad and Jack Knoll. *(Wynecoop photo)*

-Chapter 40-
A Fishing Tale

Another of our favorite pastimes was fishing. We had a wooden row boat that must have weighed a ton. We left the boat in the small lake on the road above the house all the time so the cracks would swell shut. It still leaked, so we always carried a can with us to bail out the unwanted water.

I figured out that I'd get to do a lot of fishing if I volunteered to row the boat and clean the fish. Mom helped me, but I sure cleaned a lot of perch. We pulled the skin off of the fish with a pair of pliers instead of scraping off their scales, which was a popular method at the time.

Rowing that old water-logged boat was not easy. When I rowed that tub, the tracks it made through the water looked like a snake's trail. But somehow, we always made it back to shore with all hands on board. Most of our fishing was during the summer and fall. This was more than a sport for our family, because it provided us with a lot of tasty food for our table.

Occasionally we tried fishing some of the small streams for trout, but that wasn't very productive. Uncle Glenn Galbraith and Dad talked about a good trout stream called Nine Mile Creek over on the Colville Reservation, so when the right time rolled around, we headed for the Colville. Dad didn't go this time. Just Glenn, Wig, Judge and I went on this safari.

To get there, we had to cross the Columbia River, and the only way to cross the river near us was by the ferry boat at Gifford. That was always fun, especially the first time. Once we got to the ferry landing, we had to wait for it to cross back to our side of the river. We saw it coming in a cloud of blue smoke and heard its roaring motor. The Columbia River is close to a mile wide at the crossing, so this meant a good long ferry ride.

When the Grand Coulee Reservoir was full, the landings floated high and the ferry was easily docked. There was only room for six to eight cars on the ferry. Once they were loaded on, the ferry backed out and away we went! After about 30 minutes, we docked on the other side. It was quite a treat riding on an open-air river ferry, since my only other water travel was in the old rowboat.

Once we crossed the river, Glenn knew how to get to the targeted fishing spot. It wasn't long before we had our camp all set up for the night. Glenn cooked one of his specialty meals, which usually consisted of anything we had on hand – chopped potatoes and onions, canned corned beef hash and corn. Plus, we always had a can of pork and beans on the side.

As dinner cooked in Glenn's big iron frying pan, it looked better and better. The meal may have looked pretty rough when he started, but as the many ingredients cooked slowly together, it all looked and smelled so good. Usually, a layer burned to the bottom of the pan, but that added a lot to the cookout flavor.

After dinner, we sat around the fire discussing the next day. As the evening wore on, it got darker and the sky started to cloud up. The old black clouds started to roll in, but that was okay with us, because we knew that it wasn't supposed to rain. We talked about that possibility, but since we could occasionally see a star or two, we figured that it was going to be a good night for sleeping.

We had our sleeping bags lined up all in a row on a piece of canvas and partly covered with more canvas. Just before we went to bed, we noticed a line of soft sand and gravel which would be softer to sleep on than the rocky ground under the canvas. So we moved to the sand and made a nice little nest to sleep in, then crawled into our old sleeping bags.

After we were sound asleep, the patter of rain drops woke us up. We tried to cover ourselves up with the top tarp, but it wasn't big enough to keep the four of us dry. The grass was now wet, so we couldn't move over onto it. We decided to tough it out in the ditch, thinking the rain wouldn't last very long.

But it kept coming down. Wig got up first and ran to the old International pickup with his sleeping bag. The rest of us stayed outside, because it wasn't raining that hard. We were just about back to sleep when we heard a *beep*. Then it got quiet again. After several more minutes, we heard another *beep*.

This went on for some time and we all thought Wig was hitting the horn in the pickup. After several *beeps*, it really was irritating. Judge and I were getting mad at Wig and yelling at him to quit beeping the horn. We thought he was just beeping the horn to be funny. But to us, lying in wet sleeping bags in a rainstorm trying to sleep while a beeping horn kept sounding off, it was not a bit funny.

Wig kept calling out to us that it wasn't him beeping the horn. But he was the only one there to hit the horn, so we knew it had to be him. The horn kept beeping, and we all kept yelling at each other, until Wig finally got out of the cab, opened the hood, and pulled the wire off the horn. We knew then that an electrical short had been causing the beeping that had kept us awake.

After Wig jerked off the wire, that problem was solved, and we were able to go back to sleep. I was soaked with sweat from yelling at Wig about as much as I was soaked from the rain.

We were almost asleep again when I noticed that my sleeping bag was really getting soaked on the bottom. Judge's bag was also getting mighty wet. We had to move to a different place because our nice, soft, sandy sleeping place happened to be the channel for a small side stream.

Sometime during the night, Judge ran to the pickup to join Wig in the cab. But all of those years roughing it in Alaska had paid off for Glenn, who wisely pulled the canvas over his bag. I was the only one who stayed out in the rain, with no place to go.

Since the bottom of my sleeping bag was soaked, I rolled over and slept on the drier top. But that was not much better, because it just got wet from the rain, too. What a night! It seemed like it lasted forever.

Finally it started to get light, and we were glad the rain had stopped. Since we hadn't expected rain, we hadn't covered our wood, so it was soggy. This was bad timing, because we really needed a hot fire to warm us up and to cook breakfast with. Once we finally got the fire to burn, the wet wood made mostly smoke.

Eventually, the wood dried out and we had a good fire going. We tried to dry out our sleeping bags, but soon decided that was a real waste of time. Breakfast was hotcakes and eggs, which would normally have been a great meal. But, our being up all night, wet and cold, had dampened our spirits considerably.

We didn't do much fishing that day. Everyone was tired and wet, and the brush along the creek and beaver dams was wet, too. It wasn't long before our remaining dry clothes were soaked. We finally just packed up and went home. Glenn had caught a few fish, but that morning's take wasn't worth the misery of that trip.

Chick, Judge and Wig, Uncle Glenn's future fishing partners. *(Wynecoop photo)*

-Chapter 41-
More Homemade Toys and Gun Tales

We also made a lot of our own summer toys. One special creation was our tractor. First, we took a 2" X 4" and cut three notches in one side of it, two of them deeper than the other one. Then, we knocked the wood out of the notch and had made a good seat. Next, we cut two smaller boards not quite as long as the tractor body and rounded the corners with a wood rasp. These became the tracks. We nailed the tracks to the body so that they protruded below the bottom of the body. We had made for ourselves a great play tractor. After that, we went big time into logging and road building, just like our Dad, of course.

Another clever toy was made by Dick. He took apart an old tricycle that he'd picked up at the junk yard. He removed its handle bar and front wheel and turned the body over so that the wheel ended up where the handle bars had been and the handle bar was where the wheels had been. Instead of the seat sitting high on the metal pipe between the rear wheels and the yoke for the handle bars, the seat was now low on the bottom of the curve. Dick had made the first "Big Wheel," a real going-machine.

We watched Dad use tractors to skid or pull the logs. By putting a nail in the back of our play tractor and tying a string to it, we skidded many a limb down the hillside ourselves. Then we piled them like Dad always did in his logging business.

Dad logged along the road above the house. The logging company had an old "A" frame loader to put the logs onto trucks, so of course, we built one to load our logs. Our loader didn't work too well; its strings were too big and we couldn't find a way to grab the logs like Dad's loader did.

The standard practice was that once you logged an area, you piled and burned the logging slash. So did we, except we were not as skilled at controlling the fire. We had built fire lines around our burn, but when the wind came up, the fire crossed our puny lines. The next day, Dad and some other men had to put out our fire while we were away at school.

Steve on a homemade car and Dick on his "Big Wheel".

Dick on his "Dickmobile." Behind Dick is the mowing machine and the stand of Quaking Aspen we slept in. *(Photos courtesy Phoebe Wynecoop)*

Dave on his applebox wagon. *(Photo courtesy Phoebe Wynecoop)*

One afternoon in the fall, Dad asked Wig, Judge and me if we wanted to go down to the river with him to burn some logging slash or brush. Of course, we instantly piled into the Jeep and were raring to go. Once we got the brush burning, the smoke rolled high into the air and we were having a great time.

After the brush had burned, we jumped back into the Jeep and headed home a different way. Wig was driving, zooming along on the road next to the river. Dad was in the front seat with his rifle across his lap. Suddenly, we saw something running below the road. Then it tried to cross the road right in front of us.

It was a big black bear. Wig didn't see it, but Dad and the rest of us did. Dad jacked a shell into the chamber of his .270 rifle, and with it still in his lap, he pulled the trigger.

Chick and Judge in the background with Dick and Dave in the basket. Note the toy truck in the left background. *(Photo courtesy Phoebe Wynecoop)*

Ka-Boom! What a noise! That old bear went down. Wig skidded to a stop and backed up to see what would happen next. The bear was lying below the road, and we all peeked over the edge to have a better look at it. The beast showed no sign of life, so Wig jumped down and pushed its body several times with his toe and I jumped on it. It didn't move. Then he reached down and grabbed its stump of a tail and pulled.

The bear made a slight "*woof*" sound, and Wig jumped back ten feet and hit the ground running. He just knew that old bear had him. After that one grunt, the bear never moved, so we cleaned it and loaded it into the back of the Jeep and took it home. Dad gave it to one of the local families, because our family didn't care to eat bear meat.

As I said, Dad had several kinds of rifles and did a lot of hunting. We kids hadn't graduated to larger rifles or shotguns until we were around 14-15 years old, but we were more than willing to try them out. By now, Wig was hunting deer, too.

We could go deer hunting if we were willing to drive or chase the deer in a specific direction. We started driving deer when we were only ten to twelve years old. Someone dropped us off along a road, then we headed through the woods walking towards another road, making all kinds of noise to run the deer toward a hunter waiting on a stand.

I don't think that plan worked very often, but at least we never got lost. And we learned a lot about hunting and walking through the wild woods in the process. I could carry my .22 in case I saw a grouse, but I couldn't shoot a deer.

We kids thought we just needed bigger rifles to be better hunters. We hadn't shot all of Dad's many guns yet. Of course, bigger rifles meant more recoil, and we were not sure about wanting that. We had already tried firing a 410-single-shot shotgun and that kicked pretty good. We knew we were not near ready for the mighty old 12-gauge.

Aunt Esther owned a 45-70. After we had checked it out on our cougar hunting trip, we decided that if we were going to shoot big game, that would be the rifle to use. My second cousin "Smelly," short for Melvin, was Aunt Esther's grandson.

I remember one time when Smelly had the rifle. I don't know how or why he had it, but we decided to try it out. That thing was big and heavy, and one kid could hardly hold it up by himself, but each of us was determined to shoot it. One at a time, we tried to shoulder it, but we feared that if we fired it, we would be flattened.

After much discussion, Judge and I kept telling Smelly to shoot the thing first, and then we'd try it. Smelly said, "No way! I'm not shooting that thing. It will really kick." We had to agree with him on that and after a lot of dirt-kicking and scratching around, we finally came up with a plan. We decided to tie it to two trees and then tie a string to the trigger so we could test out how hard it kicked.

We found two good trees and tied the stock with baler twine to one tree and tied the barrel to another. Smelly tied another string to the trigger and put a shell into the chamber. After several half-hearted attempts, he finally pulled back the hammer. Then, with a great yank, he pulled the trigger. The noise was ear-shattering! But more important, after the smoke cleared, we could see that the gun was still tied to the trees. We compared our visual findings and determined that the kick from that old rifle wasn't too terrible, after all. Yet, we knew that the old rifle was still an awesome piece that deserved our respect.

Since the rifle hadn't exploded and was still in one piece, we pronounced it safe for us to shoot. Next, we only had to determine who was to shoot it. Our cousin Smelly finally said he would do it. It made sense that since Smelly was the one who had borrowed the gun from his grandma, he would shoot it first.

Smelly put a big shell into the chamber, pulled back the hammer, and pulled the trigger. Much to our surprise, once the smoke cleared, Smelly was still standing. That old 45-70 sure made a racket and looked pretty tough, but it was okay to shoot after all. Then Judge and someone else shot it, but I wasn't about to pull the trigger on that big old monster. Why, I couldn't even lift it, let alone hold on and stay upright while shooting it.

Dick and his teddy bear with matching headdresses. *(Photo courtesy Phoebe Wynecoop)*

Some kids we grew up with. This photo was taken at Richard Phillips' birthday party. Left to right: Unknown, Reverend Lee's son, Yvonne Phillips, Mo Phillips, Dick Wynecoop, Richard Phillips holding his sister Barbara, Dave and Steve Wynecoop. *(Wynecoop photo)*

-Chapter 42-
Forest Fires, More Smoking and Chewing, Too

Fire was a real threat to us on the Reservation. Granddad worked up at the Agency and fought a lot of fires, but like many of the men, he was getting older. Strong, young firefighters were scarce during the war years.

Many of them were in the service, so available labor was usually pretty poor in quality and few in number. The government eventually lowered the age restrictions for fighting forest fires to sixteen, so that added two years of kids to the pool of eligible firefighters.

As a kid, when I was down in the field and the smoke rolled in from a forest fire, I'd get a queasy, nervous feeling. Fires really bothered me. I always wished I could go help, but I was too young, according to the Reservation's rules.

When unexpected smoke appeared, all of the men sixteen and older dropped everything and headed for the fire. During one big fire, a lot of airmen from Spokane's Fairchild Air Force Base were brought in to help fight it. At the time, that seemed like a good idea. We later learned that those guys spent more time sleeping than fighting the fire.

Since sixteen-year-olds were not allowed to work in the woods, Dad hired two old-timers to help with the logging. They were Tennessee Ridge-runners, and a sight to behold, chewing tobacco and slobbering everywhere. The tobacco juice ran down their chins and into the depressions in their necks, and they always needed a shave; otherwise, they were fairly clean. I don't think they ever offered us a chew, and after looking at them, we didn't have much desire to try it.

They really enjoyed telling us stories about themselves. One of them told us he would pay us if we got him some frogs because he liked to eat frog legs. There were a lot of frogs around, so we went to work with our slingshots and got him some. We took him a full coffee can of them to see what he would do next, but then he told us he didn't want them after all.

That made us mad, because we would never kill something without a

Sherwood Mountain fire lookout with kids on the rail. *(Photo courtesy Ruth Hintze)*

purpose. I guess he figured that once we got rid of most of the frogs, he could probably sleep better at night. We tossed all the dead frogs back into the lake.

These old loggers lived in what looked like a railroad box car on a trailer. Of course, their shack was without running water or a bathroom, but it was a fairly nice set up, since there were no trailer houses available. That place always had a certain smell to it – of cooking and body odor – what an awful combination.

These men worked in the woods as loggers without many problems. But their fire-fighting ability was another story. You had to be in top physical condition to fight fires, so the older men were of little to no help when we were faced with a firefighter labor shortage.

The sixteen-year-olds who were allowed to fight fires worked hard on the fire lines, but they reaped certain other benefits for their hard labor. Cigarettes were among the rations issued to the firefighters. And while the C-rations issued were considered by adults to be pretty bad, to us kids they were great! The crackers and canned pound cake were especially delicious. And we each had our own "P-38" can opener that came with the rations. Of all these goodies, the cigarettes attracted the most attention.

We didn't smoke government-issued cigarettes often, but when we did, we smoked more than one at a time. We'd light them one at a time, then fill up our mouths with eight or ten of them to be funny. Sometimes, my mouth was so full of cigarettes that I couldn't even close my lips or take much of a puff.

I can remember the many times we'd lie down under the thorn bushes and try to smoke the "C-rat" cigarettes, usually Lucky Strikes. Occasionally, one of Wig's school friends, "Windy" a.k.a. George Wynne, would have a whole package with him and we'd help him smoke them.

Chewing tobacco was really popular. Some people chewed instead of smoking. Firefighters chewed tobacco instead of smoking because they could chew all day without missing a beat. Smokers had to take a break to light up. Both Copenhagen and plug tobacco were popular types of chewing tobacco back in those days.

One time, some older kids had come over to our place. We were all down by the basement garage door talking, and one of them, named Willie Boyd, pulled out a plug of Star chewing tobacco. It was a dark, brown, small square that was so hard you needed a knife to cut it. It was possible to bite off a chunk of the stuff, but in the process you lipped the whole plug and no one wanted a bite of something another guy's lips had touched. There was something manly about cutting a slice of tobacco with a knife – a "Real Man" thing.

Well, we were all watching Willie cut off a sliver of tobacco and put it in his mouth. He cut off slices for everyone and then looked at me and said, "Well, kid, do you want a bite of plug?" I said, "Sure." So he cut off a slice, and holding it between his thumb and the knife blade, he handed it to me. I looked it over and put it into my mouth.

That chew wasn't too bad at first, but as the tobacco juice started to develop, the taste got really foul. I didn't want to spit it out, since that was not a manly thing to do, but by then I was beginning to feel pretty bad. My stomach started turning over and churning. I don't know if I looked green or white, but I sure felt like it. I was in pretty rough shape.

I went around the corner and spit out the tobacco, then I went into the house. All the big boys were laughing. That experiment ended any interest I ever had in chewing tobacco or smoking cigarettes.

-Chapter 43-
Corrals and Barns

We needed good corrals when we were branding and ear-marking the calves. We also used the corrals to hold the cattle while we sorted them before hauling them into town for sale. Dad had originally built a corral across from the house and wanted to add onto it. I think he had done most of the work on the old corral by himself.

The first corral was in a poor place and too small, but we continued to use it. The cattle didn't want to go into it, because it was near the house and they generally avoided tight places. They could be forced into a corral only with our great effort. Sometimes they would break back and at a full run, scatter us kids everywhere. Uncle Bill and his son Bob sometimes came over on horseback to help us corral the cattle.

After old Mose's house had burned, the little house next to it was abandoned. Dad bought the property, and the land provided the perfect place for a better corral. The old hay shed had been down several years and the rain and snow was ruining the hay. It was time for a major change.

Dad decided to move the cattle operations over to Mose's old place. He bought a Quonset hut from Dix Steel to use as a hay barn. When it was completed, our cattle business was moved to this new site. The new barn was a lot different to work in than the hay shed. The metal Quonset barn had no air circulation and collected heat, so it made for a real hot, dusty workplace. We tried to fill the barn as fast as possible to get out of that miserable hot box.

After we moved the hay operations into the new barn, we needed corrals to go along with it. Dad hired Smelly to help us build a series of corrals, lanes and a chute to use for loading cattle for shipment.

Because Dad wanted a big corral, we had to dig lots of post holes and cut countless poles. To make this big job easier, Dad had bought a post hole digger that was attached to a chain saw. The auger was tall, with the saw shoulder-high to the operator and his helper. Because the saw was so high, it was hard to apply pressure to make it dig deep.

A trunk full of trouble, Judge Chick and Wig on the old Buick trunk. Note the dog claw marks on the trunk. *(Photo courtesy Phoebe Wynecoop)*

We kids created a new way of getting the job done. We hung onto the handles and pulled down. The holes were still hard to dig and it really got tough when you hit a rock. If you were inside the handles when you hit a rock, the saw was so strong that it spun and knocked down whoever was trying to hold onto it. That was one tough job, trying to hang onto that auger/saw. After some scary mistakes, we learned to stand back and give the saw plenty of room.

Dad wanted us to use burned trees that had turned into pitch for fence posts because they were strong and wouldn't rot. Since these were hard to find, we used a lot of western larch for fence posts. Once we started to get some posts in the ground, we cut lodgepole pine for corral poles. There was one nice stand of good lodgepoles not far from our house. Armed with double bit axes, we cut poles and loaded them into the back of our faithful Reo truck.

After we'd dug many holes by hand or with the auger, and cut and hauled many poles, the new corral started to take shape. We built two corrals and a loading chute the first year, and added another corral later.

From the lower end of the middle corral, we added a wing that ran to the barn, and where the wing met the corral, we added a gate. When the gate was open, the wing was closed and the cattle went into the corral. If the gate was closed, the cattle walked straight through and didn't go into the corral.

This simple wing made it easier for us to catch the cattle. Once they rounded the corner past the barn, they could only go into the corral or run over anyone who was chasing them. They chose to run us over more than a few times.

With the completion of this nice new corral, we invented another game. Once the top pole dried, we'd walk the top pole around and around the corral. The corral had to be 70 to 80 feet on a side and about six feet tall, so it was just perfect for pole-walking. We were pretty good at walking that top pole, but it was not fun to fall and end up straddling it. I still think about that kind of pain and hope never to experience it again.

About the time we were building the corral, yodeling became popular, so we tried to learn to yodel. I can remember Judge holding onto the top pole, leaning back, singing a western song, and trying to yodel. He thought he was pretty good; at least he must have thought so, because he did a lot of it. I will make no further comment on his yodeling skills.

Wig and Judge in the finished corral. *(Photo courtesy Phoebe Wynecoop)*

-Chapter 44-
Hauling Hay

As I described in the last chapter, Dad had a Quonset hut barn built on the new property where we would put the baled hay. The reason he had to do this was because the old hay shed had been blown over by a strong spring wind one day while we were at school. After I got home and heard the news, I went down to examine the old thing and saw that it was really flattened. As I crawled on top of the collapsed roof, it didn't seem as big as before. It was kind of sad for us kids to see it go, because along with it went our hay tunnels and playing in the hay. The loss of the old hay shed changed our winter fun by eliminating one of our main sources of entertainment.

As mentioned before, Dad planned to buy a baler. He bought a round bale machine because it was lighter for us kids to work with and not as dangerous. In the time between when the old hay shed went down and the new barn was built, we had to stack the bales outside. It's too bad, because we lost half the hay when the bales got wet and the hay rotted. With no barn to hold them together, some of the stacks fell over and the bales rolled away. Nothing worked right for several years.

Also, stacked bales didn't allow for hay play tunnels. Bales were too hard to jump on, not soft and cushiony like loose hay. And if we broke the strings around the bales, the hay would be very hard to move. We realized that it would no longer be fun for us to play in the hay.

Hauling baled hay took more people and several extra steps. Here's how it worked. The truck driver would drive between two rows of baled hay, and someone would walk on each side of the truck to throw the bales onto the truck. With the help of a hand-carried bale hook, you snagged the bale, then loaded it up onto the old Reo. Someone on the truck stacked the bales. When we got to the stacking place, we unloaded the truck by carrying the bales or tossing them from the truck bed onto the stack where someone else did the final stacking.

Hauling hay was really hard. We were not very big or strong, and the bales were heavy. By forcing a knee up under the bale and using a hay hook, we could usually manage to swing a bale onto the truck or stack. Dad sometimes hired a couple of local kids to help. This would leave somebody free to cut, rake and bale ahead of the haulers.

The round bales usually nestled together pretty well. But this didn't always work unless the bottom bale was propped against a post or something solid. One time when we were stacking oat bales and I was on top of the stack, the bales rolled. I fell down and sat right on my bale hook. Man, that smarted! It didn't go in that deep, but it sure hurt. I hobbled up to the house and Nurse Mom checked out my latest wound and pronounced me okay. My "cheek" was a little sore for a while, but I survived.

The stacks of baled hay always started out level on top, but after some time, they tipped over. Then, when the fall rains and snows came, as I said before, a lot of hay was ruined. We tried everything to keep those stacks up – posts, poles, even a bulldozer. But none of our efforts paid off.

Dad knew that we desperately needed another barn. The Quonset hut filled the bill. We filled it with hay stacked up the sides and all the way to the top. Then our valuable hay stayed dry.

Of course, there was a trade-off. I once tried to cook an egg on the roof. The roof was round so it just slid off. Stacking baled hay in the new Quonset barn was a hot, dirty, hard job. The dust rolled in and the sweat ran off of us in sheets. The old hay shed had been pretty cool compared to the new all metal one. It was always a great day when, after the new barn was completely filled, we could stack extra bales outside in the fresh air to take their chances in the elements. We always used the bales that were stacked outside the barn first.

Hauling baled hay was a totally different game than moving loose hay. Round bales had to be carefully loaded, and the ride had to be smooth and even, or a calamity might develop. One hay field was some distance from the house, and like all fields, it was fenced and gated. To get from that field to the Quonset hut, you had to go through an obstacle course – up a hill, past some big trees with limbs that stuck out into the road, and then through the gate.

The gate had to be kept closed because of stray horses and cattle. So, when we pulled up to the gate, someone had to jump out and try to run ahead and open it without causing any delay. That runner didn't usually get it open in time, so the truck driver had to stop. Once the gate was opened, as with all stick shifts, the truck rolled backwards, stopped, and then jerked ahead when it got back into gear.

One time, an especially uneven load of hay rocked back and forth too many times. Then, as the truck started up the hill, the limbs from the trees shifted the load backwards. The combination of jerking truck and tree limbs pulled the load and kids completely off the back of the truck. Down we went, screaming kids, bales, and dust. No one was hurt, but it was quite a thrill to be knocked off a truck with a load of hay.

By now you know that the old Reo truck served many purposes. We used it to haul hay, wood, cattle to market, ice skaters, huckleberry pickers and many other things. By family tradition, most of the driving was done by the oldest kid. His seniority didn't automatically ensure his good driving skills.

We never had any vehicle accidents, but that poor truck sure took a beating. Hauling hay was the hardest work we gave it. It's a wonder that the transmission survived its many drivers. We quickly learned that if you let out the clutch and stepped on the gas too hard, you had to re-load the hay.

Shifting down was the hardest. Everyone did what was called double-clutching. That task took good timing – and required speeding up the motor, and stepping on the clutch, and shifting to a lower gear – all at the same time. Any halfway-experienced driver could effortlessly complete this operation. We got better with practice, but in the meantime, the poor transmission suffered a lot.

With us kids at the controls, if we were successful, the rest of the crew usually gave a loud, sarcastic cheer, "Yea, about time!" That old Reo was one tough truck; a lesser truck would have left a trail of gears down the road, given up and died.

Steve and Dick playing with toy equipment. Anything to do with vehicles of any type was a great pastime. *(Wynecoop photo)*

-Chapter 45-
Sleeping in the Bushes

We always had some loose hay around and put it to good use as matting for our nights out. It was great to take our blankets outside and lie under the stars and tell stories until we fell asleep. Once, when Lee and Stanley Rima were helping us with the haying, Lee told us a tale about a cougar. He said that a real live cougar once jumped up onto their house and they could hear it *purding and purding*, also known as purring and purring. Supposedly it was making its nest to sleep on their roof. That story was too much. We laughed all night long.

Once, we cleared a place in the thorn bushes and quaking aspen stand across from the house. Then, we found some old bed springs and hung them in the bushes. Once the springs were level, we piled our blankets on them and slept swinging in the trees.

It was really fun to sleep out there, but it always got so cold in the morning. We really could have used more padding under us on top of the springs. When that early morning cool air came up from underneath, we nearly froze. We never complained to the folks about how cold we were, because we thought the house was too hot for sleeping, and we'd rather have the fun of freezing while sleeping outside.

"The hot house." It seemed like the only time the house was cool enough for sleeping was when there was snow on the ground. *(Photo courtesy Phoebe Wynecoop)*

-Chapter 46-
Graveyards, Outhouses, Uncle Roy and Halloween

With the new corrals and Quonset barn in place, we changed the route of our trail to school. We no longer needed to use the high bridge, and the tree house had been broken apart by the wind which caused the trees to sway. Since we didn't need to carry water anymore either, that old trail was abandoned.

Our new path took us straight across the field behind the house, across the creek, through the barnyard, across another creek along the old road, below the graveyard, through the trees, across the road, and up the hill to school. The total distance was only about a mile, but as my kids say, "it was all up hill both ways!" Of course, the small, old graveyard was a special attraction along the way. It sat on a small hill overlooking the family farm and provided a good place for looking around. While there were no certified ghosts in residence, we knew that the opportunity was always there for some to materialize.

In general, we didn't like spending much time in the graveyard and seldom went there without a good reason, such as a burial. We avoided those. But it was fun to visit it every so often just to read the tombstones and check the names, dates and inscriptions, especially for relatives we remembered or for someone we heard talked about.

Halloweens were filled to the brim with our naughty deeds. We would hide in the trees near the graveyard. All our activities were after sunset. We went trick-or-treating to get food (apples, cookies, candy) or other goodies. We sometimes carried a flashlight, depending upon whether or not there was any moonlight. Then we just wandered around for a while, munching on our loot and throwing sticks into the road. There were so few houses to go to that we ate all of our treats as we collected them.

Of course, knocking over outhouses was the premier prank for Halloween rascals. Uncle Roy LeBret owned the local general store, and his public outhouse was always the first to go over. Actually, we never got to tip it over ourselves, because someone always beat us to it.

To some folks, Uncle Roy was a bit of a character. For one thing, he dug a basement under the store with an old Fresno (a small earth moving tool that when pulled behind a tractor, collected loose soil or dirt). Then he filled the Fresno with dirt manually with a shovel and pulled it out from beneath the store with the tractor. All the kids said he was like a gopher, since he was always under the store – so we nicknamed him "The Gopher." Since he was really a nice guy, we never let him know about his nickname.

Uncle Roy had another attribute we talked a lot about. He always seemed to have a drip on the end of his nose that was ready to fall. It was fascinating to watch him go about his business in such a state. The drip just dangled there, dangerously, poised and ready to fall.

This was especially fascinating to watch while you were ordering a pound of sliced lunch meat from him. You see, back then, lunchmeat came in large rolls and had to be sliced, usually by hand with a knife. While he was cutting the meat, we intently watched to see when and if the nose drop would fall. I never saw it fall on our lunchmeat, but I knew it must have at one time or another.

Uncle Roy always ran his arm by his nose while he was cutting the meat and he kind of talked to himself, saying, "Yup, yup, and a loaf of bread." We laughed about it, and he laughed and carried on, too. I always will wonder where the nose drop went when it wasn't wiped off before my very eyes.

One Halloween, Uncle Roy decided to defend his targeted public toilet. He built a fire and stayed outside with his outhouse until the danger was over. That's dedication. The next year, Smelly set the toilet on fire right after school, before Uncle Roy was ready to defend it. Of course, everyone knew who had done the dastardly deed. At the time, it was really hilarious. But once Smelly was caught and had to pay for the damage, it wasn't quite so funny.

Halloween was especially great on full-moon nights. When the moon was extra bright, we stayed out extra late – at least until 8 o'clock. Of course, we usually added to the chill in the air by re-telling "Walt's White Thing" or some other ghost story.

We never wore costumes or masks on Halloween. We dressed to stay warm and yet light enough to run fast when necessary. The tribal police tried to find and catch all Halloween vandals, but we always got away by running through the woods. They must have forgotten that we were only doing what they had done when they were kids. Why, our own Dad told about once helping to put a cow on the school roof one Halloween night. Another time they tied a cow to the church bell rope. That bell rang all night long. We never dreamed of achieving that level of prankdom.

To put a cap on our mild-by-comparison traditional Halloween escapades, we walked part-way home with Jim Wynne, who lived out past the Ghost Rock I mentioned earlier. Coming back past the rock wasn't too bad, because the moon didn't shine on it from that side. If you ran fast enough, you could get past it before the ghost could get you.

The LeBret/Galbraith store and post office in Wellpinit.
(Wynecoop photo)

-Chapter 47-
Ponds and Rafts

The ponds in the meadow caused more than a few problems for us kids. One spring day, Mom was standing at the kitchen sink looking down toward the meadow. She suddenly said, "Are those kids in the pond?" Looking down there, I had to agree with her that that is what it looked like. She told me to go down and tell them to get out of that water before they got sick. Down I went to check it out, and sure enough, Dick and Steve were playing in the pond. The pond water was freezing cold, but the air was warm, probably about 50 degrees.

I was only there a few minutes, when here came Mom, right behind me. You could tell she was furious! She had a switch in her hand. Steve got out of the water and put his shoes back on, but Dick was still in the pond. The closer Mom got, the farther out he went. She told him to get out or she would spank him. But he refused to get out, and she wasn't about to go in after him. They finally compromised. Mom promised not to spank him if he got out. She put the switch down and headed back for the house. After she had gone a ways, he came out of the pond.

Dick was sure that Mom was coming back, so he stayed close to the pond until she was all the way back to the house. She never said a thing at dinner that evening about the episode. It was obvious that she was still mad, but her word was good, as always.

That little pond in the field wasn't the only pond that caused problems for us. There were several natural ponds above the house, but they were supposedly full of blood-sucking leeches. To avoid feeding the leeches with our blood, we dug our own swimming hole.

On the trail to the barn, the nearest creek was fair-sized. It came from up the draw above the culvert where we got our water and it ran all year. The water was cold there, like in the pothole lakes above the house that filled with water every spring. Of course, that signaled it was time for us to build rafts. There was one major risk with our raft-building idea. We couldn't swim. Fortunately, the natural ponds were only waist-deep and the water was clear. Later in the year, they were full of grass so we built our rafts early in the season.

Our first rafts were made out of wet, heavy aspen logs that had fallen down and laid on the ground all winter. It took us all day to build just one raft, because we didn't have the best material. The wood was so wet, it couldn't float if it had to. We tried wiring the rotten logs together, and wasted a lot of Dad's nails, nailing them together, but nothing really worked. After just several trips, our rafts started to come apart, making them very difficult to stand on. Once a raft was in the water, that is where it stayed, because it was too heavy to pull out. The logs were so wet that they didn't float, so our feet were also wet from standing on the slowly sinking raft.

For all our time and effort, we only got wet and cold. Finally we wised up and started using drier logs. But we soon learned that even these better rafts sank if you left them in the water for several days.

Once we had a raft that would actually float, we went out onto the pond or lake and drifted around. With the help of a long pole, we could go explore the whole lake. That was always a great time, yelling and laughing about our great fortune – finally getting a raft to float.

Usually our fun soon turned into hard work, because the raft didn't float very high on the water. Weeds and grasses got in the way. And there was always another danger lurking if you accidentally fell into the water where the dreaded hungry leeches waited for a meal. We were never bitten by the bloodsuckers, but the idea that they were there kept us high and dry. The water was so cold, that the leeches were probably frozen.

The alternative to playing on one of our homemade rafts was the old wooden boat that was regularly left soaking in one of the lakes. Dad didn't like us to use that decrepit boat, but once in a while it would somehow get loose and drift out, full of kids on an adventure. Boats get loose all the time. Most, if not all, boats were wood, so they were stored wet.

-Chapter 48-
Swimming

We had a summer game we played with Dad. We waited until he was reading or about half asleep, then we asked him to take us swimming. He'd grunt a half-hearted, "Okay." We'd run and get ready. Then we had to remind him that he had agreed to take us swimming. After some growling, he'd finally take us.

The only safe place for our water play was down at the Spokane River or at Tshimakain Creek about 10 miles from the house. Those spots were safe in one way, but dangerous in another, because there were always rattlesnakes near the water. We seldom swam in the Spokane River, because it was like a sewer. The water was covered with a green scum and really smelled.

Every Fourth of July, we went down to the creek for a picnic and to swim. Family picnics were very common and we had several during the short summer. Even in mid-summer, the water was so cold there that it was hard to get in. And there were only a few holes in the creek that were big enough for swimming.

As we grew, we needed a larger place to swim, so we decided to dig our own swimming hole near the house. We started planning a much bigger pool than the one we ended up with. Working at it in our free time, we took several weeks to dig that swimming hole. We soon found out that digging and throwing dirt was pretty hard work.

Once the six-foot-long by four-foot-deep and four-foot-wide hole was dug, we diverted the creek into it. We were so proud we had created our own private swimming pool.

The stream that fed our swimming pool ran through the corral, so the water was really dirty. In fact, the water was so nasty that I always thought we were dirtier getting out of the water than we were before we went in. But that was the least of our worries. That very dirty water was also extra cold. One reason for its iciness was that we had dug the hole in the shade

Chick, Judge and Wig at "Muscle Beach," Loon Lake style. *(Photo courtesy Dorothy Tandy)*

of a big pine tree, so the sun didn't heat the water at all. Once in the water, we couldn't stay very long.

The bottom of our pool was ankle-deep mud and the edge of the pool

Wig, Janet, Vern, Judge, Dick and Chick swimming in Tshimakain Creek. *(Photo courtesy Robert Wynecoop)*

was also muddy. Once you crawled out of that place, you were covered with mud. We had worked so hard at digging that swimming hole, we didn't want to give up on it, but after one short season, we did.

Once we were able to drive, we went to the larger lakes to swim and fish. The top two feet of the lakes were warmer than the stream water and our "swimming pool." At first, I didn't like the big lakes because I needed the security of being able to touch the bottom. Basically, I was afraid of deep water, and I didn't want to learn how to swim in it. I just knew I was going to drown, for sure. We often talked about how Louie Eli had drowned while trying to swim across Turtle Lake.

When you're learning to swim, you kick and paddle so hard, thinking that you will eventually just start swimming. But that didn't work for me. I turned the water into a froth, and still I couldn't swim. After a while, I eventually figured it out and it became so easy that I wondered why it took so long for me to learn how.

I believe I was the last of us boys to learn how to swim. After many years of frustration, at age fifteen I just started swimming one day. What a relief! That was a big load off my back and mind.

We built a diving board off the rocks at Turtle Lake. Some of the kids liked to dive off the rocks into the water. Once I was a swimmer, the older kids accepted me into their group. I jumped off the board a lot, but the other kids spent more time diving and swimming than I did. Although I had finally learned how, swimming was never my thing. It was fun and cooled you off, but there were too many other things I'd rather do – like join the 4-H Club, where you could keep your feet planted on solid ground.

-Chapter 49-
The Electric Club and the B-29 Crash

We kids belonged to the 4-H Garden Club and to the Electric Club. The Garden Club required you to do a lot of record keeping, like describing how you prepared your garden plot, what seeds and fertilizer you used, etc. We also recorded our hoeing and weeding efforts. I hated the record keeping part of gardening.

Growing a garden was easy where we lived – except for the dreaded weeding. We helped Mom a little with her garden of potatoes, carrots, onions, radishes and flowers. But we probably didn't do a very good job as gardeners, since we always grew more weeds than edible produce.

Washington State 4-H meeting. First row from left: Chick Wynecoop, Squeak Tandy, Philip Wynecoop, Marlene Wynne, Janet Wynecoop, Esther Lowley. Second row: Sara Wynecoop, and other delegates from Stevens County. *(Wynecoop photo)*

The county fair was in Colville, 80 miles away, so we didn't prepare an exhibit to enter there right away. First, I had to win at the local fair before I could enter the county fair. We did put on an exhibit of fresh vegetables and a board with an electrical wiring display at the local fair and Pow-

Wow. The local fair paid more prize money than the county fair did, and we were satisfied with that challenge. We always won a couple of dollars. Once, I did get to the county fair, not as an exhibitor, and I had a lot more fun there enjoying the carnival rides and side shows than looking at the exhibits.

The Garden Club was a mixed group of boys and girls, while for some reason, the Electric Club was all boys.

The Electric Club always met at Mr. Tandy's. He was our fearless leader. Once we had finished the project for the day and the meeting was over, we all went outside and played Kick-The-Can well into the evening. We had so much fun kicking that old can.

Once caught, you were *it*. That meant you had to cover your eyes while standing by the can and counting to twenty while the others hid. If the hiding kids could sneak back and touch the can or kick it, they were *in free*, but if you saw someone, or you out-ran them and touched the can first, they were caught and became *it*. However, if someone not caught beat you to the can and kicked it, everyone went free and the game started over. At this point, they only had the time it took to recover the can to hide. This was a fast, wild, high-energy game.

One hot August afternoon, as we were working on our Electric Club project, we could hear an airplane overhead. Since the war was over, airplanes were a fairly common sight. There were two military air bases nearby. Spokane Air Depot or Air Force Base, now Fairchild Air Force Base, was a B-29 base. Geiger Field was a joint fighter and civilian airport.

But this particular plane we heard that day seemed to be making more than the usual amount of noise. We often used any old excuse to get out of finishing our assigned electric project, so we asked to go out to look at the loud airplane. Mr. Tandy eventually gave in and we all went outside to have a look.

It was a lazy, summer day with cotton-ball clouds in the blue sky. That plane was crossing high and a little to the east of us, but we could tell that something was wrong. It was trailing white smoke! That B-29 was on fire! Behind the airplane, we saw small white puffs that were *not* clouds. They were parachutes!

We all just stood there, mouths open, wide-eyed and all ears. Each parachute had a small black dot swinging underneath it. We watched them until they disappeared into the trees about five miles away.

The airplane was still flying, but all of a sudden, an engine fell off one side and the plane tipped to the other side. After the motor fell off, the plane went into a steep dive towards the Spokane River, south of town. While in its final dive, one more parachute appeared behind it. Not too long after the airplane went behind the ridge, a big cloud of black smoke rose up. The crash was too far away for us to hear it. We had counted a total of eleven parachutes either in the air or already on the ground. Man, what a day! A burning B-29, parachutes everywhere, and a big cloud of smoke! That was the most exciting Electric Club meeting we ever had.

Since late August is right in the middle of forest fire season, and the firefighters were already on alert, all of the available men gathered and went to see where the plane had crashed.

While this was happening to us and the firefighters up near the Agency, Wig was back at our house. As soon as he saw the parachutes, he jumped into our Jeep and went looking for the men who had bailed out.

So many things were going on at once. All us kids were watching the adults load up bulldozers, shovels and other fire fighting tools and head for the fire that was billowing black smoke.

Within about an hour, Wig arrived at the Agency with a bunch of airmen and parachutes. No one had been injured, except for scratches and bruises. Then Wig went back for more.

In the meantime, the rolling cloud of smoke was getting bigger and really boiling. Since we were all too young to help, we just stood there and took in all the excitement and tried to stay out of the way. More and more people were coming in and signing up to fight the fire, because it was still growing, not weakening.

A line of airplane fuel had spread from the motor impact site to where the airplane had crashed about a mile and a half mile away. Scattered fires burned between the two sites, and since the wind was blowing, the fires quickly spread together and on up the cheatgrass hillside.

By now, all eleven of the parachuting airmen had been recovered. But we later found out that one person who had not bailed out was lost in the crash. He had been going out the door when the engine fell off the plane, and as the plane tipped, he was probably knocked back into the doomed aircraft. That was terrible news. In our quiet little world, this was enough excitement to last us quite a while.

Early the next morning, the fire was finally brought under control. Wig took us down to the airplane crash site, which was close to the road and easy to see. The military personnel had cordoned off the area until the airman's body was recovered. Weeks later the area was partially covered with soil and we were allowed to walk around the impact site.

Like everyone else, we picked up a few souvenirs. There wasn't much left, because the military investigators had taken all the large, important pieces. Wig had a big piece of the propeller, but like many other family souvenirs, it has disappeared over the years.

Next, Wig took us up to see where the motor had landed. Parts of it were scattered around there for a long time. We picked up a lot of small cable. Wig made our biggest find – a parachute, complete with parachute cords made of strong nylon. We tried to use the parachute for a tent and a few other things, but that didn't work out very well. Eventually, some of the local women took it and made clothing out of it.

I probably don't need to say that when the burning airplane came over and crashed, we didn't get around to playing Kick-The-Can that night.

When I got home, everyone had a story to tell about the day the B-29 came down. The events of that afternoon gave us enough excitement to last a long, long time. Yes, I did grow up a bit more than usual that day – befitting my new blue shirt, belt and hair style.

I had worn a new blue shirt to the Electric Club meeting that fateful day. I thought I looked pretty good in that shirt, and I had hardly been able to wait 'til I could wear it. Wearing that blue shirt made me feel great – not because I wanted to impress the girls, because there weren't any in the Electric Club – but I thought it just looked good on me. By now, I was almost thirteen, and I had grown a little, especially in the hips. When school started, I was going to wear pants *with a belt.* A new blue shirt and pants with a belt – man, I was growing up! To top it off, I had started to comb my hair like the older boys, with a little raised flip in front. In more ways than one, I was coming of age.

The airplane engine crash site. This photo was taken in 2003. Some evidence of the crash is still visible, including small parts of the aircraft. The arrow points to part of the wreckage. *(Photo courtesy Robert Wynecoop)*

-Chapter 50-
Political Conventions

In 1948, I first became aware of political conventions via the old reliable radio waves. For some reason I was just fascinated with them. Back then, conventions were more fun to listen to than they are to watch now on TV. My imagination made the event seem bigger than life. The roar of the crowds and the politicians' speeches were the greatest. I was especially caught up with the delegates' voting.

As they cast their votes, if there was a question about a vote, a delegate would rise and gain recognition and then ask for the delegation to be polled. Someone would read off the names of the questioned state's delegates and they, in turn, cast their vote. This went on until they went through the complete list of delegates for the state being polled and got everyone's final vote.

The conventioneers groaned loudly together when a delegate requested a poll of the larger states like New York, Pennsylvania or California. The man calling the names slowly went down the list until everyone had voted, and then they moved on to the next state, hoping no one would question the vote count and request a poll. What a process, and so exciting to me!

In our family, Mom and I were the only ones interested in the political process. We just knew that Dewey would be elected as the next President, but somehow Truman won. What a surprise! I had listened to how both candidates had been nominated, then I followed the campaign as best I could until the big day of the election. I couldn't wait until I was old enough to cast my vote. My first opportunity to vote was in 1956, eight long years later, when I helped to elect Eisenhower.

-Chapter 51-
Eating Meals, "Wild" Snacks and P.J.

Our evening meal, which we called dinner, was usually eaten at the dining room table. You were expected to be there on time, when the meal was put on the table. Other meals, breakfast and lunch, were taken at the kitchen table, since we were all coming and going on different schedules, except during the summer haying season, when the hay crew sat at the table.

There was always time to get your chores done before it was time to eat breakfast. Breakfast was somewhat different from dinner, because it was spread out over a 30 minute period to allow for the amount of chores and other work each of us had to do before school. But, if you didn't finish your work and you were close to the house, you could eat when the food was ready. School started at 8:45 A.M., so we were up and at our chores by 7:00-7:30 A.M. We usually left for school by 8:15, after breakfast.

Let me tell you, there is nothing like crawling out of bed on a cold morning, going downstairs, sitting at the table and eating a bowl of hot oatmeal with whole cream and toasted homemade bread covered with wild strawberry jam. We often had pancakes, bacon or ham, and occasionally, we ate French toast or cold cereal.

By this time, we no longer had a dairy, so the old separator had disappeared. Our old cow was milked twice a day, so we had more than enough fresh milk to make our own butter, which we did by either shaking a jar full of cream or by using a butter churn. Making butter was hard work – it took a lot of shaking or churning. Mom drank the pale, gloppy, buttermilk, but I could never bring myself to try it, no matter how much she encouraged me. We used the rest of the cream on other kinds of foods like hot and cold cereals and desserts.

To get cream, we just put each day's fresh milk inside the refrigerator, and by morning, the cream rose to the top of the container. Once the cream had risen, it was ready for cereal. My favorite combination was Wheaties and cream so thick it could hardly be stirred. Man, was that good! Corn Flakes were a distant second favorite, but not nearly as tasty as "The Breakfast of Champions." I still think about those delicious breakfasts, but don't eat that way anymore –too much fat and cholesterol.

One weekend morning, we were all eating a big breakfast of hotcakes, eggs, and bacon. I was sitting next to Dad. We all had a place at the table and you usually sat there. I sat on Mom's left, but this time I was on Dad's left. He reached over and took a piece of bacon off of my plate. I didn't say anything, and everyone started to give me a hard time. Then I said that it was okay for Dad to take that meat because I had just choked on it myself. The moans and groans were pretty loud from all sides of the table. Dad gave me a funny look. By then, he had already swallowed my chewed-on bacon.

We also ate a lot of toast. Mom's toast was really special. She heated up the sliced, buttered bread in the oven, then we added homemade jam or jelly on top. That was so delicious. During the war, when supplies were limited, we spread lard on bread, then sprinkled sugar on top. That sounds pretty gross today, but really, it was very tasty. Try it.

We were expected to act like gentlemen at the table and we had one rule that could not be ignored. At all times you must have one foot on the floor.

Our favorite evening snack was a bowl of oatmeal. We did our own snack cooking, so there was always a lot of cream added to whatever we made. Another one of our favorite original treats was bread-in-milk. This was not hard to make at all. We simply tore up a slice of bread and put it into a glass of milk. Since Mom baked all of our bread, our bread-in-milk was especially tasty and filling.

We also ate a lot of wild meats. We were one of those meat- and-potato families, so we ate some kind of meat at most dinner meals, often for lunch, and occasionally for breakfast.

Dad sold all the beef we raised because it was a money crop, so we lived on venison and grouse. Venison steak rolled in flour and fried, mashed potatoes and gravy, and some other vegetable, corn or peas, was our standard dinner fare. To top it off, we often had cake, pie or some other homemade dessert. Ice cream was hard to keep at home, since we didn't always have a freezer.

You can probably tell by now that we produced most of our own food. We had a garden, hunted and fished, picked berries, baked bread and desserts and had a milk cow. We only bought a few things when it was necessary.

Right after the war, a new boxed product came out called margarine. Inside of the box was a bag filled with a real sick-looking white-colored substance that looked like lard. Also in the box was a tablet that you mixed into the white stuff, and the tablet eventually turned the margarine a weird yellow.

In a year or so, the coloring was enclosed in the margarine bag. You had to rupture the coloring button, then knead the bag until the coloring was evenly mixed into the margarine. It took a lot of work to blend it all together. At first, everyone wanted to be the one to mix in the color, but after a while it became just another chore. Squeezing that bag for twenty or thirty minutes was hard work, about as hard as making butter. All of the effort produced a bag of yellowish-orange pasty margarine that tasted okay, but nothing tastes like real butter.

About this time, we stopped milking the cow, so we had to buy and use the new margarine. We also had no more fresh cream. That was quite an adjustment for us to make. We had been spoiled all of our lives by eating fresh butter and cream.

One of our strange food habits was that we kids liked to snack on raw potatoes. They were really crunchier and tastier than cooked spuds. Across the creek, along the old trail to school, was a patch of potatoes that someone had planted for several seasons. If we were hungry on the way to or from school or to the store, we'd stop and dig up a fresh potato, wipe it off in the grass, and eat it raw. We were careful to dig our snacks from different mounds, so the owner didn't know we were enjoying his spuds. Since our trail went right through the middle of the potato patch, we had a lot of spots to choose from. Our trail pre-dated the potato patch, so we felt we had squatter's rights.

Just past the potato patch, several apple trees grew that belonged to the government employees who lived at the Agency. Since those folks never bothered to pick the apples, and no one else did either, we also occasionally snacked on a few juicy apples as we were going and coming along the trail. The apples were so hard they were difficult to eat.

Sometimes our friends would stay for dinner. One kid we all called "P.J." essentially moved in with us for a while. P.J. lived with his grandparents and had no one his age to play with, so he spent all his time at our house. He had little to nothing of his own except for his little dog named Smarty. Our folks helped him a lot. They bought him clothes to wear to school, but someone took his new clothes.

P.J. and Smarty spent many days at our house just doing whatever we were doing. P.J. was not a bit bashful about being "adopted" by our family. He even joined in and helped us with our chores. It was too bad that he moved away when he was eight to ten years old. We found out later that he was killed in an accident. He was like several other kids, bounced from one family to another.

Lorena Knoll and Wig sampling peas from Grandad's garden. *(Photo courtesy Phoebe Wynecoop)*

-Chapter 52-
Hotshot Slingshots

As I previously mentioned, we played with just about everything we could find around the place. Our "toys" were usually things we had made ourselves. At church, we had heard the story about how David had used a rock in a sling to kill Goliath. Naturally, that gave us ideas. We talked to Dad and found out how easy that type of sling was to make. Here's how.

First, you take two shoelaces and the leather tongue out of an old shoe, cut a hole in each end of the tongue, then tie the laces to the tongue. Turn the tongue so it forms a cup. Next, you put a loop in the free end of one of the shoelaces, and put your first finger through the loop. The other shoelace you hold in the same hand.

By holding the laces up high, you put a rock on the tongue or now-pocket. As long as the pocket is soft enough to hold the rock, you can hold the strings and spin the rock around in the air. When you reach the desirable speed, you let go of the loose end of the string, and the rock now becomes a projectile. With practice, you can really whip a rock around and throw it at a good speed a long way. Of course, that happens only if you let it go just right and have some specific idea about where you want it to go.

One evening, we were all down batting the rocks from the gravel pile that had been dumped below the house to be used as a leveling course under the yet-to-be-poured concrete slab in the basement. Somehow, that gravel pile got smaller every night. We were using the smaller rocks as ammunition for our slingshot practice. Aiming for a tree or rock, we were trying to improve our accuracy for grouse hunting. We were all in sync, except for Judge. He was whipping rocks around with his sling, just hoping to hit anything, anywhere.

I do not know how David ever managed to hit Goliath, even though he was a good-sized target, being a giant. It must have taken a lot of practice. Judge was practicing a lot that night, but as I said, his rocks were landing wild.

Well, Judge let another one go, but his rock didn't go very high, and it hit the bed of the old Reo truck. In one bounce, it crashed right through the truck's back window. All activity stopped. Everyone held their breath, wondering what would happen next.

Judge turned around and looked at Dad with that "I-really-did-it-this-time" look on his face. Everyone waited to see what Dad's reaction would be.

Dad said, "Damn it, Judge! If you can't do any better than that, throw that thing away. Here, let me show you how." Judge handed him the sling, and Dad put the string around his finger and a rock in the pocket and started to swing the sling around his head. Once it was swinging fast enough, he let it go. *Bang* it went, off the truck bed, *thunk*, right through the same now-broken window. Just like Judge! We all almost died laughing! Dad could have never done that again if he tried, but he sure did it that night! Dad handed the sling to Judge and walked up to the house in silence. Years later, when we finally retired the old Reo truck, it still had those two rock holes in its back window.

Ike, the dog, is sitting in the Jeep. The Reo and Ford truck with a load of hay are in the background. *(Photo courtesy Robert Wynecoop)*

-Chapter 53-
Baseball

Most of that rock and gravel pile, intended for other purposes, ended up on the far hillside. In addition to providing slingshot ammunition, those materials were used every evening for batting practice. We'd toss a rock up in the air and hit it with a stick when it came down. We busted and batted rocks by the hour.

One of our projects was to mark off our own baseball diamond in the field behind the house. That home field was smaller than a standard sized baseball diamond, but it was complete with a pitcher's mound and all the bases. When other kids came over, we'd play baseball until the ball would start falling apart.

Baseballs were few and far between, so after it got to be in real bad shape, we just taped it back together and played another game. We only had one bat. No one was big enough to break it, so we played a lot of baseball with our one bat and one baseball.

When Steve was young, I remember him lying in the grass watching the older kids play softball. One time, the batter hit the ball right towards him, so he hid behind a little bush. But the ball bounced over the bush and hit him right on the nose. That must have really hurt, plus his nose started bleeding, so he had to go into the house – wounded.

Back then, there were very few left-handed baseball players. Since I was a *south-paw*, Dad wanted me to be a pitcher. I tried pitching, but I really didn't like it. During my high school years, I did some pitching for the Wellpinit Redskins, but I quit after that. Dad sure had some high hopes for me, but I wasn't big enough to throw a good fast ball.

As one of the few left-handers in grade school, I had to wear a right-handed thrower's baseball glove on the wrong hand. Of course, the fingers didn't match up, and that was a real handicap. Dad eventually bought me a glove to wear on my right hand. That glove was strange. It had a thumb and only three fingers, not four fingers, like today's gloves have.

High school baseball team, 1952. Back L to R: Jim Wynne, Thomas Sam, Carson Sherwood, Kenneth Eddy, Albert Brown, Coach Glenn Galbraith. Front L to R: Chick, Judge, Bud Peone, and Mel Peone.*(1952 yearbook)*

Town team in 1958, Wellpinit style. Front row: Dave, Wig and Judge. Back row: Steve, Chick, Vern and Dick. *(Wynecoop photo)*

I also learned to bat right-handed, since there were no lefties to learn from. I didn't set any batting average records.

Our school played other schools during grade school and in junior high. In one grade school game against Fruitland, I made a triple play. They had no outs and runners on first and second. I was playing second base. The batter hit a line drive right to me. I caught it for one out, touched second for the second out and tagged the sliding runner for the third out. Thanks to poor base running, I had made a triple play! That was a shining moment in my baseball career – not bad for a kid my age.

One rainy day, we were playing a baseball game against St. Maries Junior High in Chewelah. I was pitching, and the pitcher's mound was really slick. I wasn't wearing baseball shoes, so I was sliding all over the mound. On one pitch, my right foot slipped and I threw the ball right over the backstop and out into an adjoining field. Not many can make that claim to fame. That was not a shining moment.

Playing baseball at the grade school and junior high levels taught us that we could compete against bigger schools. That we did, and for us, size didn't count, so we usually held our own against the other schools.

When we were not playing on the baseball diamond at home, we had batting practice, using a homemade invention. We stretched a telephone wire tied high up in one tree down to another tree some distance away at about belt high. To this, we tied a piece of loose wire with an old baseball attached to its end.

Every time we hit the baseball, it slid up the wire and then came back down. We hit it again, and it went back up the wire. This worked smoothly once in a while, but usually the ball came back swinging and bouncing down the wire, making it a very hard target to hit. We spent a lot of time trying to make that batting wire work better, but we just couldn't stretch that old telephone wire tight enough.

Another option for building up our batting skills was to bat a lot of rocks around with anything that was handy. I don't know how many ax handles or other sticks we beat up, but we smashed more than a few bat substitutes.

We also played a lot of a game we called "500." One person would hit fly balls or grounders, and whoever ended up with the ball would get points based on this scoring system: 100 points for a fly ball, 75 points for a one-bouncer, 50 points for a two-bouncer, and 25 points for anything else. Of course, if you made an error, you lost points the same as you'd gained them. The first player to reach 500 points became the batter. Of course, we were very gentlemanly in the way we played. There was never any pushing or shoving – just a lot of bumping and crowding. The quickest scrambler usually got the ball.

Also, Dad taught us another fun activity. By using a string on a long stick, we could throw an arrow a considerable distance. First, we tied a knot on the end of a string. Then we notched an arrow made of a straight piece of any kind of wood. Next, we put a nail in the front of the arrow to make it fly straight and to give it weight; otherwise, the arrow would just flutter, not fly. Using this method, we could whip an arrow a good 100 yards. Of course, just like with our rocks and slings, it was pure luck if we hit what we were throwing at.

After the war, when all the servicemen and other families came back to the Reservation, everyone played baseball. All the communities had baseball teams for adults. These teams practiced twice a week and played games against other teams on Sunday afternoons.

When I was 9-12 years old, I was the batboy for our adult team and that was a lot of fun. I traveled with the team to all the nearby towns for games, usually with my Aunt Amy and Uncle Merritt. I had my own uniform, and took good care of the bats. During those years as batboy, I learned a lot about the game of baseball and about competition, too. I thought that it was great how everyone played so hard against each other to win the game, but stayed friends after the game was over. Baseball was a fun sport, but it was also serious business on the Reservation.

-Chapter 54-
Spokane Trips

As I mentioned before, Dad was also in the logging business, so he had tractors and bulldozers. Like all mechanical equipment, they occasionally broke down. When this happened, he had to go into Spokane for parts. If we were not busy with chores or some other activity, and could get ready quickly on short notice, we got to go with him. Since he usually waited until after dark to head for home from shopping, that allowed time for us to take in a movie in a real movie theater. We especially enjoyed the cartoons and news that ran before the main feature.

If we were in school, Dad usually made the Spokane trips alone or sometimes Mom went with him. I remember one particular time when they had gone into town together. Mom had left us a note saying that if we frosted the angel food cake she had made we could have some. Angel food cake was a real treat for two reasons: they were hard to make and they took a lot of eggs.

Mom probably thought we'd eat the cake anyway, so she might as well have put the frosting on it first. But she made one fatal mistake. She didn't tell us how to make the frosting.

Once everyone got home from school, the great debate started on how to make the frosting. I thought we should mix milk and powdered sugar together. That argument won for a while, but we used too much milk and the frosting was real thin.

Judge played his famous line, "Since I am the oldest, I know better...and I say we have to add cornstarch." That helped the frosting to thicken some, so we added more cornstarch and flour. By now, the frosting was pretty thick. Since we had a lot of frosting, we decided to fill the hole in the center as well as cover the cake with this pasty concoction.

The cake looked pretty good all covered with frosting, and we each cut ourselves a well-deserved slice. But oh, that frosting tasted horrible! We scraped it off the cake and tried to feed it to Tex, our dog, but even he wouldn't eat it. Now, if Tex wouldn't eat something, that was pretty bad. Unfortunately, we'd wasted a lot of powdered sugar. That wasn't good at all, especially since sweets were so scarce in those days.

As I said, Judge, like older brothers, always thought he knew better. That was usually okay with the rest of us, because he then was responsible for whatever the results were. Mom wasn't too happy about the cake frosting and we rightly blamed Judge for the overdose of cornstarch.

Sometimes we went into Spokane for sporting events. I remember one special time when we watched Joe Louis fight Tiger Jack Fox in a exhibition match. Judge and I were running around in the bleachers at the Spokane baseball park. When Tiger Jack Fox came out of the locker room and entered the ring, the crowd cheered. We ran down to see him walk by. Joe Louis, the then-heavyweight boxing champ, came out next and walked right past us. Man, was he big – bigger than life! Unfortunately, the fight wasn't much. They mostly just pushed each other around. But one of my claims to fame is that I did see Joe Louis box – live.

Dad was also a wrestling fan, so sometimes he and Granddad went into town to take in the wrestling matches. If we were lucky and were all caught up with our work, we could go along. Those wrestlers were really something, especially Gorgeous George. They all had colorful costumes and fancy robes, but George was really something to behold. Atlas was another favorite wrestling personality who was fun to watch, along with many less famous wrestlers. These guys would strut around the ring in their costumes as the crowd cheered them on, but once they took off their robes, they were not so big by today's standards. A 200 pounder was considered a big man in those days.

Occasionally, we would go into Spokane to shop for school clothes or a winter coat, or something else we needed. If we timed it right, we ate downtown at the Chungking Inn, a Chinese restaurant, or if the Chungking Inn was full, we ate at Travos, a sit-down restaurant.

Like all kids, we liked to listen to recorded music. If you wanted to listen to a certain song at the Chungking Inn, you could go over to a window and request it. Or you could talk into the box at your table to someone in the back room to make a request. I remember sitting in a booth and requesting a song, Number A-16, by talking into the speaker. I was so nervous that I forgot what song I wanted and just blurted out a number. I guess whatever song came out was okay with me.

One day, after we finished lunch at Travos, we were waiting to pay the bill. Near the entrance was a machine that some people were playing. Watching them closely, I could see that when someone put in a nickel, things started to move around inside the machine. Since I had a nickel, I went over to try my luck. I reached up and dropped the coin into the slot and pushed the button. As expected, things started moving. When everything stopped moving inside, twenty cents dropped into the little cup on the front on the machine. Of course, I wasn't supposed to be playing that machine, but that was a minor problem to me, considering that I had made fifteen cents playing a pinball game.

Just like today, some of the Spokane radio stations played requests. Our favorite station was KREM, which played country music. We listened almost every night to see if anyone we knew would have a song played for them. Of course, it would have helped if we had sent in a request once in a while. We never did that. Still, we were devoted KREM listeners. That station is still around today, but there aren't any request programs.

Both of those restaurants are gone now. They have been replaced by today's fast food style eateries.

-Chapter 55-
The Telephone

By November of 1945, our family numbered seven boys: Wig, Judge, Chick, Dave, Dick, Steve and Vernon Wade. Dad was doing very well in the logging business and in many ways, the times, they were a-changing. About this time, the government, with Dad's encouragement, decided that it would be in its best interest to hook our house into the government telephone system.

We were not far from the main telephone line, so it didn't take long for the fireguards to run the telephone line down to our house and install a telephone inside. Our phone number was one long and three shorts. Man, we were now big-timers – we had our own telephone! We didn't have private lines in my younger days. Everyone was on a party line.

The wall-mounted phone box was made of wood, with two bells with a small metal ball on a rod between them that vibrated back and forth, causing the phone to ring. A rotating handle on the right side of the box was used to get it going (cranking it up).

There was a cone-shaped mouth piece in the center of the box that was attached by a short stem that could be moved up or down to fit the speaker's height. A 24-inch covered wire came out the left side of the box and a cone-shaped receiver was attached to the other end of the wire for hearing the person at the other end of the line. A U-shaped hook was also attached to the left side, and when you placed the ear piece receiver into the hook and released it, you had hung up. The line was then open for others to use.

To call someone, which we rarely did, you'd pick up the receiver off the hook to see if someone was on the line. If no one was talking, you'd simply crank the handle on the right side of the box until you heard the appropriate number and types of rings. You'd ring their number once, twice, three times at most. If no one answered, that was the end of that – you just didn't talk to them. Imagine using that kind of telephone today!

Dad goes big-time in Lumberman's Magazine.

Kids didn't use the phone then. We survived not having to talk to each other. A telephone was a business necessity, not a social disease like today.

The operator's number was one long ring, the Agency was a long and a short ring, and the code was different for every family who shared our "party" line. Some nosy people listened in on all telephone conversations.

It sounds funny now, but back then, that's what the gossips did – listen in on other folks' telephone calls. We called that kind of snooping "rubbering" (short for rubber necking, which was a common name for those who listened in on others' conversations by stretching their necks to listen).

Having telephones in our homes really opened things up for us. We didn't feel so isolated anymore. We had joined the rest of the country. Occasionally, people would come to our house just to use the phone. And having our own telephone soon became a real necessity for running Dads' business –for ordering parts, setting up meetings, etc. No other area family had a phone since it was a government line.

The telephone came in handy for other things, too. Dad fought a lot of forest fires and had a crew of experienced men working for him, including his older brother Bill. Since they usually needed to rally on short notice, that new phone really helped with speeding up emergency situation communications.

In the summertime, we were cautious about using the telephone if there was a thunderstorm booming around. When we heard the first clap of thunder, we knew that the telephone was off limits. Anyone talking on the phone risked getting a severe lightning shock.

Several times when the lightning struck the telephone line, the electricity actually raced down the line and into our house. A ball of electricity shot out of the telephone, bounced off the living room wall, then it disappeared. Lots of people said that such a phenomenon was impossible. But we had seen it happen enough to know it wasn't. That ball of lightning that visited our parlor added an extra dose of excitement to a good old everyday thunderstorm.

After we'd been zapped by lightning several times, we wished that phone was long gone. We called the Agency about our problem. They finally listened to us. When one of the older telephone technicians came down and checked the phone, he made an amazing discovery. The installers had not put a fuse in the line to prevent such striking events! Anyway, we always gave the telephone a lot of room during thunderstorms, even after the problem was supposedly fixed. Even today, many folks never use the telephone during a lightning storm.

Early telephone usage instructions. *(From the book: Thomas H. Elsom, Spokane's First Telephone Installer by Dean Ladd)*

-Chapter 56-
Tex Does His Thing

Uncle Bill, Dad's brother, occasionally did logging work in the woods for Dad. Smaller and older than Dad, he was kind of feisty and seemed to enjoy hassling his younger brother. One Saturday morning, we heard some commotion out on the front porch, so I jumped out of bed, dressed and ran down the stairs and out onto the front porch. There was Uncle Bill, griping to Dad about something. By then, he was more than complaining – he was really bitching up a storm. Naturally, we kids all gathered around to hear what was going on. Our dogs were wandering around, paying good attention, too.

Bill was really getting warmed up, now that he had a young audience of kids and dogs. Our old dog Tex walked over towards Dad, and then over to our uncle.

Then Tex started sniffing Uncle Bill's leg. Since Bill had a ranch and dogs, we all thought that Tex was just checking out the scent of Bill's dogs. That's what Uncle Bill thought, too. But Tex had different ideas. He kept sniffing Bill's lower bibbed overalls pant-leg while the loud talk went on and on. All of a sudden, Tex hiked up his leg and peed all over Bill's lower pant leg and boot.

When Bill realized that Tex had peed on him, he jumped up, half kicking our dear, fearless dog, who by now was running down the steps off the porch. Bill just stood there a minute, then said, "Damnit Wynnie (Dad), you have been peeing on me all your life, and now your dog does it."

Bill stomped off of the porch, got into his car and took off in a cloud of dust. I am sure he could hear us laughing all the way home. Tex really knew how to end a conversation! I swear that dog was smiling when he scurried down the porch steps.

Uncle Bill and Dad weren't always on such poor terms. Dad's big brother had horses and occasionally helped us with marking and cutting our cattle.

His son Bob was good-sized, and an experienced cowboy-rancher as well as a professional rodeo bronco rider.

When it came to cowboy skills, the kids in our family were too small to take down a calf. We tried more than a few times, but a three month old calf is pretty heavy, and the calf always won the match. We could rope a calf, but then we usually got dragged around the corral until someone helped us out of a bad situation. Anyway, pretending to be cowboys was all like fun to us. While Uncle Bill's kids considered themselves to be real cowboys, and they were, that was a title I did not ever care to claim for myself.

Tex, the culprit standing in front of Wig and Judge. (Photo courtesy Phoebe Wynecoop)

-Chapter 57-
Spring on the Spokane River

One sunny Saturday spring morning, some of us were talking about how nice it would be down by the river. The longer we talked, the better it sounded. We also had other thoughts about going somewhere else, but the more we deliberated, the better the river sounded. I believe we even told the folks about our plans this time. Then, away we went. We were too young to drive so we walked.

We packed up and toted along several .22 rifles, a couple of bread rolls and some candy bars. To get there, we had to walk about five miles, and we passed many houses on the way. Eventually, we passed Charlie Flett's house that sat high on the hill above the river.

We started down a rocky old cattle trail that led to the riverbed, but after a short distance, we headed off on our own into the rocks and worked our way down to the road at the bottom of the hill. Along the way, we rolled rocks down the hillside. It was fun to watch them send up a big splash when they hit the water. To get to the river, the rocks had to cross the road. But, since there was usually no traffic, no one was hurt and nothing was damaged.

By the time we reached the river, we had eaten all our food and we needed some water since we were thirsty. Pretty soon, we felt like we were dying of thirst, so we had a drink from a small creek, where the water tasted nice and cool. After we had drunk our fill, we wondered where that water had come from. Then we realized that the stream ran through several barnyards on top of the hill. All of a sudden, knowing that didn't leave us with a very good taste in our mouths.

But since the sun was out and the weather was warm, and we had gotten overheated in our heavy coats, we decided that the water from the stream had probably saved our lives. All things considered, we decided that we could live with it.

We spent another 20 minutes throwing flat rocks to watch them skip over

The Spokane River, upriver from the sand slide. *(Wynecoop photo)*

Downriver from the sand slide. *(Wynecoop photo)*

The Spokane River. *(Courtesy Northwest Room, Spokane Public Library)*

the water's surface. The Spokane River's water surface was really flat since it was part of Lake Roosevelt, the resevoir behind Grand Coulee Dam. Then we looked for arrowheads along the riverbank. Finally, we started heading for home. Once again, we were very thirsty. We knew there was a clean spring that ran up by the road, so we cut up and across the hill and headed for it. Now, that water was truly pure and tasted delicious.

Beside that spring there was an old cattle watering trough made from a hollowed out log. This leaky old log created a long pool of water for cattle or horses to drink from. Outside of and at one end of the trough was a short culvert standing vertical with its base buried in the ground.

Water fed constantly into the culvert, which was always full of spring water. The excess water was piped into the trough. The water came into the culvert with such force that it bubbled out of the top, to the delight of everyone drinking from it. When it really gushed, your face was washed and your thirst was quenched.

We always chose to drink out of the culvert. After all, who knew how many cows had drunk out of the trough, let alone walked in the water. The water boiled up so strong that all the kids called it "Coyote Slobber." For some reason, that name stuck, and for ever after, Coyote Slobber was the name of that particular spring.

Unfortunately, someone decided to fix Coyote Slobber's fresh bubbles and completely ruined it forever. Progress is its own worst enemy. They took a bulldozer to it, and now there is little to no water at our favorite fresh watering spot.

As we walked along the road going home that afternoon, several cars and pickups passed us, but for some reason, no one offered to give us a ride. Eventually we made it home, tired from our long day's hike. Lucky for us, Mom had baked fresh bread. There was nothing like her homemade bread, butter and wild strawberry jam. That treat was the perfect ending to a great day.

Enjoying spring on the river became the thing to do. The snow always melted down there long before it did by our house. We spent many a weekend on the river rolling more rocks, playing on the sand slide, shooting woodchucks, or just enjoying the sun.

After WW II ended, Dad bought a Jeep. If ever there was a more perfect vehicle for a bunch of kids than a Jeep, I don't know what it could be. Wig drove, and the rest of us sat wherever we could, and away we went! Of course, this was long before anyone thought about wearing seat belts or taking any other safety precautions. Somehow we stayed alive.

We spent hours joy riding everywhere in that thing. It was also our serious hunting vehicle, but it was especially great in the springtime to roar along

Wig, Vern, Dave, Judge, Dick, Steve and Chick in the perfect kid machine. *(Photo courtesy Phoebe Wynecoop)*

the river with the top off, looking for woodchucks to shoot at just for fun. We covered every inch of that riverbank and drove every road or old cow trail on our end of the Reservation in that Jeep.

One fall day, we were riding in the Jeep down by old Jackson Elijah's garden. We had heard that coyotes had been eating his watermelons, so we decided to play good Samaritans and help him out. We loaded up the back of that Jeep with watermelons and took them up to Jackson's house. He was real surprised when we delivered them right to his front door. He laughed and thanked us.

The river's sand slide was the most fun. It was at least one-third of a mile long and just steep enough for great rock rolling, too. We spent hours on that slope, digging out rocks and watching them roll down the hill and into the water. Sometimes, as the rocks rolled down, we'd fire off a few shots at them with our rifles.

Sometimes we'd hear a *whing* sound, meaning we'd hit our target and the bullet had ricocheted off, just like in Tennessee Jed's radio program. Jed was a sharpshooter who specialized in high accuracy and zinging bullets. But we didn't indulge in rock-shooting often, because ammunition was too precious to waste on rocks.

Sooner or later, we kids usually ended up at the bottom of the slide. Since the sand and gravel was too loose to climb on that steep slope, we had to go around the end and climb up the long way, which was definitely the easier way. That was a real workout climbing the long hill up from the river.

We also gathered old tires, loaded them into the back of the Jeep, and headed for the river. During the war, there were not a lot of extra tires around, so we usually ended up with the discarded ones that had not been burned up on our already-described ice skating adventures.

We rolled these ruined old tires down several hills...again and again and again. The better tire-rolling hills were the ones where we could drive down and pick up the tires afterwards, haul them back to the top, then roll them down again. Once tires were rolled down the sand slide, they went into the water and disappeared forever.

Those were such fun times playing at the river. But we also spent a lot of time working near the river, since we now moved most of the cattle down there every spring. First, we branded and earmarked the stock not already marked. Dad's brand was an inverted V over a W. His earmark was a W on the tip of the animal's right ear. By checking these marks, we knew which rancher owned each animal.

After the livestock was branded, everyone mounted a horse and herded the cows and steers toward the river. We kept the older calves back to sell, or just to separate and wean from their mothers.

By late summer, we had repaired or built new corrals on the flat above the river at Little Falls. Then we rounded up the cattle again, marked the new calves, and cut the young bulls.

We tried to improve our herd's bloodlines and only used registered bulls. The bull calves were not registered, so like most ranchers, we castrated all of them.

One excuse we gave our folks for getting to the river often was that we needed to go check on the cattle. And we did haul a lot of hay to the river to feed the cattle before the grass was tall and thick enough for them to graze on. Hauling hay to the river became real work, not like just going to check on the cattle.

Also, believe it or not, we had some rustler problems. With someone keeping an eye on things down there, fewer cattle were stolen. Dad and other adults patrolled the river roads at night, and we kids covered the roads during the day. Several times, a U.S. Marshal stopped at our house. He and Dad always went outside to talk about the problem.

For years Dad had a Deputy U.S. Marshal's badge so that he could deal with any situation directly if it should arise. None of us ever caught a rustler in action. We heard that the marshal had nabbed one, but I cannot verify that as fact.

"Checking on the cattle" usually ended up for us as a day well spent shooting groundhogs or woodchucks. We always had a .22 rifle handy, so we'd be ready to climb up into the basalt rocks for small game hunting.

Springtime meant the wildflowers were blooming all over the hillsides where we played. They were covered with balsam-root or sunflowers, buttercups, bluebells, Easter lilies, and wild Syringa, and too many other varieties to name. That was a great place to play. When the water level behind Grand Coulee Dam was lowered, we looked for arrowheads. We searched the riverbanks where the wave action from the year before had changed the shoreline. We hunted for arrowheads just as a fun thing to do. No one thought about collecting them. It is illegal to pick them up today.

-Chapter 58-
Movies Here and There

I mentioned earlier that we had cousins who had been in the military service, several of them relatively close to us in age. Once they returned after the war's end, they were no longer satisfied with staying around on the Reservation. Cousin Art LeBret especially liked going into town to see a full-color movie in a real theater.

One day, Art asked Judge and me if we wanted to go into town to see a movie with him. The folks agreed to let us go and of course, we were more than pleased to accompany him. We went in early, found something to eat and drank a mug of cool root-beer at the Triple XXX Drive-in. Then we went to a movie theater and watched a double feature. That was the first of many trips we took into town to see the latest on the silver or colored screens.

If we didn't get to see a double feature, we went to two different theaters so that we could pack in as much movie watching time as possible. Our favorite kinds were westerns, science fiction thrillers and the new 3-D movies.

Those great movie trips got us to thinking about the world outside of our Reservation. Our world was really expanding with these cinema glimpses of faraway places and new faces.

We also saw many movies in our small town of Wellpinit. Watching movies at the high school was also fun. Uncle Glenn started teaching at the high school after the war, and as a senior class fundraiser, he started showing movies there for the whole community to enjoy. Twenty to thirty people of all ages came to these showings.

On Friday nights, we rearranged the tables and chairs in the school's lunchroom into a theater set up. After everyone was seated and settled down, then the movies began to roll. Most movies were two-reels long and at the end of the first reel, the lights came on. There was a break while the film was re-wound and the other reel was loaded onto the projector. After the last reel was shown, the lights came on, the film was re-wound, the lunchroom was reset for school activities, and we all went home.

Usually, we kids walked home afterwards. On dark nights with no flashlight, our creek crossing could be a real nightmare. Later, our high bridge solved that problem somewhat. But depending on the kind of movie we had just seen, we were often in various states of fear and trembling. Our vivid imaginations ran wild while we hurried home in the dark.

Mom with her kids who loved movies. L to R: Chick, Judge, Dave, and Wig. Mom is holding Dick. *(Photo courtesy Phoebe Wynecoop)*

-Chapter 59-
While the Folks Were Away

Our folks started taking winter vacations during the early fifties, luxuries they had not enjoyed earlier in their lives. While they were away, they had an older lady come and stay with us. Mrs. Lynn was our favorite sitter. She either stayed at our house all the time or came over early in the morning and left in the evening after dinner.

Dad (Clair) and Mom (Phoebe) on a well-earned vacation. *(Photo courtesy Phoebe Wynecoop)*

Either way, we had our chores to do. One of our jobs was to keep the fire in the furnace burning. And that was quite a job, because the fuel wood was big, heavy and hard to handle. Usually, the oldest one of us kids had to get up during the night and go down to the basement and fill the furnace to keep the heat coming through the night.

Mom and Dad sent us cards from different places they visited like Phoenix, Yuma, New Orleans and Rabbit Pass in Colorado. That's how we followed the progress of their travels and got even more glimpses of the world out there.

Occasionally, they called us to see how things were going or to let us know about a change in their plans. Since we were busy with our chores, going to school, and trying to keep the house going, we didn't have much time to worry about their being away.

-Chapter 60-
Dad Becomes a Pilot

After the war, Dad decided to become a pilot. His good friend Joe Andrews was a pilot. Dan, an ex-Navy pilot, was his instructor. The three of them spent a lot of time talking about airplanes and flying. That's how Dad got the flying bug.

Dad took the necessary flying lessons in Spokane at Felts and Calkins fields, then he applied for and was granted a pilot's license for small aircraft. Once Dad had his license, he bought an old TaylorCraft, a two-person aircraft that had a wide wingspan and was good for slow flying. Dad kept it at the Deer Park airport, about forty miles from our house. This facility was a World War II bomber base, with long airstrips which made landings very easy.

Dad's plan for the TaylorCraft was this: When a tractor or any other piece of machinery broke down in his logging operations, he'd drive to Spokane, buy the necessary equipment or part, drive to Deer Park, put the purchase in the airplane, fly it out to the job site, and if possible, drop it with no parachute to the waiting crew. Then he'd return the plane to Deer Park and drive home again.

This system didn't work as well as he envisioned it would, so he decided that since he owned a lot of land, he would just make a landing strip below the house and keep the airplane there. Everyone agreed that this was a good idea.

He leveled a strip of land. Joe Andrews had no problem landing the old TaylorCraft on the field. It was all pretty amazing! The airplane sat on the ground for a while. Then, since Joe was the more experienced pilot, he was elected to take the plane back up. TaylorCraft's were not very powerful, and the new strip was short, probably too short. We were all standing along the strip watching and arguing about whether the plane would be able to lift off or not.

Down the strip Joe and the plane went. The grass was pretty tall and the wheels had just started to clear the grass, when we all could see something sticking out of the grass at the end of the strip. We did our best to lift the plane with our thoughts and prayers, but those were not enough. One landing wheel hit the protruding handle of the disc, a piece of farm equipment resting at the end of the strip.

The plane bounced and came back down to the ground with a couple of jolts. The landing gears on the plane had to be repaired, and it took some time to get it fixed. Dad had an aircraft mechanic bring out the parts and repair his beloved airplane.

Once it was repaired and the strip was cleared of grass and discs, Joe was again elected to be the fly guy. He started up the plane's engine and headed into the wind – and away it went. Again, all of us supporters and critics were standing along the strip watching and worrying. This time, we saw the wheels clear the grass, and the plane became airborne, flying free and clear. What a big day that was for Dad!

That was the only time that strip was used. Dad wisely built another longer strip a quarter mile farther down in the field, which he used safely for years. He eventually traded the older TaylorCraft for a Super Cub, which he traded for a Tri-Pacer, which is still in the hangar to this day. Wig and Dick also eventually became pilots, and if so- inclined, Dick could still make use of that old landing strip today.

Since Dad was always interested in flying, we went to air shows at the Deer Park airport and to Spokane Air Force Base, which was later re-named Fairchild Air Force Base. The pilots always put on quite a daredevil show there to thrill the spectators. Like all kids, we also had fun examining the airplanes we remembered from World War II days. The B-29 was especially interesting for us, since it was the type of plane that had crashed near our home.

-Chapter 61-
Home Movies

Since we all loved to watch any kind of movies, Dad bought a sixteen-millimeter movie camera and projector. Whenever he was in town, he rented short movies and sometimes regular length movies for us to watch at home. We watched those movies so many times, especially during the winter, that they should have been worn out. We ran the cartoons forwards and backwards and almost died laughing – especially at the reversed action.

When the Korean War started and the draft board was back in business, everyone on the Reservation was being called to serve in the military. It was almost automatic that everyone from the Reservation was drafted and would end up in an Army infantry unit.

To avoid this fate, Wig joined the Air Force and was sent to Japan and then on to Korea. Since he was in the Air Force, he did not get involved in any ground combat. He was a teletype operator and spent time in Korea and on an island off the Korean coast. When he returned, he married Janet Clinton, his high school sweetheart. He completed his military life in New Mexico.

Wig and Vern. *(Photo courtesy Janet Wynecoop Paul)*

When Wig was leaving for Korea, Dad wanted to take a silent movie picture of him. When Wig got into his car, everyone who was watching the "silent" movie swore that they heard the car door shut. We played the movie several times, and that door slamming sure seemed to be there.

By the time Wig went off to the Korean War, things were really changing at home. All of us were starting to grow up, and with Wig gone, Judge became the oldest and the leader of the pack. When Judge also went into the Air Force, I became the oldest kid around and was responsible for conducting our home-base operations.

The folks had been talking about something called television and how it would be available in our area in a year or two. We looked forward to getting a television, since it would be the first Hi-tech device to come along in a while. And we looked forward to the new adventures it would bring us, right inside our house. We also hoped that some day, we would go on to college. Those two things – television and education – would definitely change our lives. Just like we imagined the door slamming in our home movie, we tried to visualize what the new world with television would be like. We knew major changes were coming, unlike our imagined slamming door. Little did we know how much this would be true.

Wig with Vern, before leaving for Korea.
(Photo courtesy Janet Wynecoop Paul)

The Wynecoop family, posing for a photo. Back row: Dick, Dave, Chick and Steve. Front row: Judge, Mom, Vern, Dad and Wig.
(Photo courtesy Phoebe Wynecoop)

As of the date of publication, the original nine family members have gone through the following: Clair passed away in 1969; Phoebe is 94 and still living in the family home; Wig passed away from lung cancer in 1986; Judge is still logging and lives with his wife Tina in Colbert, Washington; Chick is retired and lives with his wife Lois in Spokane; Dave passed away from heart problems in 1985; Dick is ranching and lives with his wife Kay on the Spokane Indian Reservation; Steve and his wife Jeanette have a bed-and-breakfast in Redmond Washington; Vern died in a traffic accident in 1980.